5-7-73

PRAYER
IN A
SECULAR WORLD

PRAYER
IN A
SECULAR WORLD

Leroy T. Howe

A PILGRIM PRESS BOOK
from United Church Press, Philadelphia

The scripture quotations are (unless otherwise indicated) from the *Revised Standard Version of the Bible*, copyrighted 1946 and 1952 by the Division of Christian Education, National Council of Churches, and are used by permission. Biblical quotations marked NEB are from *The New English Bible,* © The Delegates of the Oxford University Press and the Syndics of the Cambridge University Press, 1961. Reprinted by permission.

Library of Congress Cataloging in Publication Data

Howe, Leroy T.   1936-
  Prayer in a secular world.
  "A Pilgrim Press book."
  1. Prayer. I. Title.
BV210.2.H67   248'.3   73-321
ISBN 0-8298-0248-7

United Church Press
1505 Race Street
Philadelphia, Pennsylvania 19102

1751128

CONTENTS

FOR NÁN

INTRODUCTION

The concerns of this book were first addressed during an interterm course conducted at Perkins School of Theology entitled "The Secularization of Consciousness and the Possibility of Prayer." Originally, I proposed the study for two reasons. In the first place, I had become intensely preoccupied with the crisis of belief characterizing much of contemporary secular culture, which now has come to haunt the churches as well. That a new mode of consciousness has emerged in Western civilization which is rapidly becoming global in scope is widely conceded by philosophers and theologians of culture alike; one cogent implication is that thoughtful participants in the present world order will continue to experience difficulty maintaining interest in and loyalty to traditional forms of Christian belief and life. The strain of living in two worlds is felt especially keenly within many seminary communities, often to the surprise of church people who usually know better. Secondly, I was coming to the conviction, which I seem to hold more strongly with every passing year, that the contours of unbelief within Christendom are revealed most clearly at the level of devotional activity, both individual and corporate. For a time, churchmen may delude themselves about the depth of their unbelief through sophisticated theological ploys justifying every sort of hesitation in the name of an otherwise thoroughly defensible outlook: pluralism. But if they are honest with themselves at all, they will recognize unmistakably their true stance of unbelief at least at those moments of great expectation in the church's ongoing life —Advent, Easter, Pentecost, say—times at which the obligations to worship and pray reappear as ominous challenges to ingenuousness. It cannot be denied, of course, that there are still countless numbers of practicing Christians who have become profoundly skeptical of traditional Christian beliefs but who contrive to contemplate, meditate, and even pray. For many, however, devotional exercises of these sorts reflect only a denial of that world which the secular mentality does more or less adequately understand, an otherworldly endeavor in the least flattering sense of that term. It is to these latter that this book is primarily addressed. The difficulties which these men and women experience, not merely with engaging regularly in devotional activities but, more importantly, with seeing them even as serious possibilities, bring sharply into relief the degree to which the power of religious affirmation may diminish as the present age becomes even further secularized. Prayer is a peculiarly distressing matter for anyone suffering the demise of his will to believe; why this should be so is one of the issues to which the following chapters are directed.

The reader will need to be wary of the peculiarities which of necessity accompany a "professional" theologian's approach to such a subject. In the first place, I do not presume to bring to the discussion insights gleaned from special competence in the practice of prayer; there is no good reason for any reader to suppose that a theologian prays more easily or adequately than others within the Christian community. (Not altogether without justification, one might be so perverse as to suggest that what in fact obtains is an inverse relationship between theological expertise and piety.) Hence, I cannot anticipate that a deepening of prayer life should result for readers of these pages; it may be the case, however, that the *possibility* of prayer will be entertained more seriously as various objections to it, secular and otherwise, are overcome. Secondly, because I develop the argument deliberately from the point of view of a Christian theologian, the reader is advised not to expect unusually perspicuous illumination of secularity at other than those junctures at which secular man, whether inside or outside the churches, finds himself in various sorts of quandary over Christian faith. It is the collision of secular mentality with faith, and not the phenomenon of secularism as such, which is to be the subject for investigation. As a consequence, the exposition is brought forward with a specific kind of person in mind: the thoughtful contemporary individual who, for a variety of reasons, some good and some bad, is not yet prepared to abandon the faith of his fathers but who finds the symbols of that faith increasingly remote from those by which he is coming to orient his life creatively in the present.

For helpful advice on the practice of prayer, what is required is a saint's vision and not a theologian's. And for an exhaustive account of secularism, a philosopher of culture is the indispensable resource. As a theologian, I am concerned with the phenomenon of prayer as one dimension of the faith whose understanding it is every theologian's task to facilitate. My examination of prayer is one expression of the comprehensive theological task, *fides quaerens intellectum.* Though theology does indeed seek an understanding of all things, because the all-sovereign and all-loving God after whom it inquires is the creator and sustainer of those things, its primary concern is with them only as they pertain to faith and not in themselves. The theologian's expertise comes into play only within, though at the outer boundaries of, the circle of faith and the possibilities beyond it over against which faith must establish its claim to be heard.

The following chapters constitute an attempt to gain an understanding of prayer as one essential response of faith to divine revelation which has come to be inordinately difficult because of certain postulates which faithful people find mandatory for the ordering of their experience in the contemporary secular world. The exposition will deal only with secularity as a problem for prayer and not secularism as such; of this limited terrain, however, a completeness of interpretation will be attempted. Although one constructive aim is to enhance the possibility of prayer for those whose thinking cannot be other than secular, no theologian can presume on the basis of his own insights to elicit the initial interest in praying, as he cannot presume to evoke faith itself. What I hope to accomplish is the more modest task of providing a reasonably clear account of what those factors are in the secular point of view which seem to impede articulation of faith through prayer, and how secular-minded Christians might overcome obstacles hindering a lively faith which is both fully responsive to peculiarly contemporary insights and grounded in the historic witness of the Christian community in all places and in every age.

In pursuing the inquiry, I have been encouraged and sustained by my colleagues on the Perkins School of Theology faculty, who comprise what surely must be one of the most caring communities of faith and learning assembled anywhere. To Professor James White, who gave the manuscript a close reading and cogent critique, I am especially grateful; whatever deficiencies remain are fully of my own perverse devising. Mrs. Bonnie Jordan typed the several drafts with astonishing efficiency and patience. My wife, Nan, and daughters, Jennifer and Allison, continue to make our home a joyful place in which to live and work; their faith, hope, and love are an enduring inspiration.

CHAPTER 1

PRAYER
AND SPEECH
ABOUT GOD

The secular Christian, experiencing several kinds of perplexity about devotional life traditionally conceived, encounters repeatedly a judgment upon his every quandary in the life of Jesus, one who to all outward appearances had no significant difficulties with prayer whatever. The "pioneer of faith," Jesus is preeminently a man of prayer, who believed seriously in the possibility of praying without ceasing. How the content of Jesus' faith, exemplified in his prayers, collides with the contemporary secular world's quandary about belief in God is the subject of this chapter.

JESUS AND PRAYER

Jesus' specific teachings about prayer seem to have been provoked by his disciples' expressed need for instruction. As they began to contemplate the scope of their looming responsibility for continuing Jesus' ministry, their thoughts must have turned increasingly to pondering what resources would be available to sustain them through the difficult times which gradually appeared to lie ahead. Always sensitive to the moods and needs of his disciples, Jesus assumed the burden of preparing them accordingly. At Luke 11:1-13 occurs the most helpful account in the New Testament of how Jesus provided his disciples with an understanding of both the principles and the practice of prayer:

He was praying in a certain place, and when he ceased, one of his disciples said to him, "Lord, teach us to pray, as John taught his disciples." And he said to them, "When you pray, say:

"Father, hallowed be thy name. Thy kingdom come. Give us each day our daily bread; and forgive us our sins, for we ourselves forgive every one who is indebted to us; and lead us not into temptation."

And he said to them, "Which of you who has a friend will go to him at midnight and say to him, 'Friend, lend me three loaves; for a friend of mine has arrived on a journey, and I have nothing to set before him'; and he will answer from within, 'Do not bother me; the door is now shut, and my children are with me in bed; I cannot get up and give you anything'? I tell you, though he will not get up and give him anything because he is his friend, yet because of his importunity he will rise and give him whatever he needs. And I tell you, Ask, and it will be given you; seek, and you will find; knock, and it will be opened to you. For every one who asks receives, and he who seeks finds, and to him who knocks it will be opened. What father among you, if his son asks for a fish, will instead of a fish give him a serpent; or if he asks for an egg, will give him a scorpion? If you then who are evil, know how to give good gifts to your children, how much more will the heavenly Father give the Holy Spirit to those who ask him?"

—Luke 11:1-13

What is striking about this passage is its representation of the practicality of Jesus' teaching: Jesus imparts knowledge of *how* to pray before he addresses the decidedly theological question of *what* prayer is. Competent and inspiring a rabbi as Jesus appears to have been, he seems never to have been tempted, in spite of his learning, to lapse into mere theorizing about the manifold dimensions of the religious life. Unlike the procedure of this book,

Jesus gives an exemplary prayer first and then an interpretation based wholly upon the example, representing his deepest understanding of prayer as address to and communication with God. For Jesus, the fundamental fact about the One who is addressed in prayer is God's readiness to hear and to answer human petitions; Jesus' God is an intimate conversation partner who remains always solicitous of his creatures' good. To be sure, there are other dimensions to Jesus' prayer life which point out other truths about God. Jesus repeatedly offered praise and adoration to that Most Holy One; he expressed gratitude both for his own earthly existence and for the covenant established by the Most Holy One with mankind on behalf of the created order; toward the end, contemplating the impending outcome of his ministry, Jesus' prayers assumed the tone of submission: "Not my will but thine be done." Only confession is absent, as would be appropriate for one who "knew no sin." The richness of Jesus' prayer life, however, ought not to obscure his crucial stress on the possibility of petition and intercession before the Almighty God in behalf of oneself and of other creatures who also may be in need. Jesus assures all and sundry that they may address God in the full expectation that every earnest request will receive a hearing. God's response may not be according to human expectation, perhaps because petitioners are not always ready to bear the cost to themselves of an answered prayer; for example, what would his neighbor think if God *did* make one more loving of those whose skin color is different? However, that *some* response will be forthcoming is guaranteed by nothing less than the divine providence itself; God has given his own promise to supply both spiritual and earthly benefits. Though Luke's account tends to stress the former, the New Testament as a whole does not in the least minimize the worldly character of the divine-human transaction. For example:

13

Jesus answered them, 'Have faith in God. I tell you this: if anyone says to this mountain, "Be lifted from your place and hurled into the sea," and has no inward doubts, but believes that what he says is happening, it will be done for him. I tell you, then, whatever you ask for in prayer, believe that you have received it and it will be yours.'

—Mark 11:23-24, NEB

Indeed anything you ask in my name I will do, so that the Father may be glorified in the Son.

—John 14:13, NEB

'If you dwell in me, and my words dwell in you, ask what you will, and you shall have it.'

—John 15:7, NEB

He did not spare his own Son, but gave him up for us all; and with this gift how can he fail to lavish upon us all he has to give?

—Romans 8:32, NEB

We can approach God with confidence for this reason: if we make requests which accord with his will he listens to us; and if we know that our requests are heard, we know also that the things we ask for are ours.

—1 John 5:14-15, NEB

In speaking of God's promises, Jesus expresses his most profound insights into the nature of God's presence in human life. Jesus' is a message about God's availability, his constant and abiding love. Jesus' prayerful addresses are self-consciously offered to the One who both sets the stars in their courses and who always stands ready to draw near to nourish man; God's closeness is Jesus' good news. In *Jesus and the Word*, Rudolf Bultmann put this point strikingly:

The recorded words of Jesus about prayer deal almost entirely

14

with prayer of petition . . . it cannot be doubted that when Jesus urges prayer of petition, *petition is meant in the true sense*, that is, prayer is not to bring the petitioner's will into submission to the unchanging will of God, but prayer is to move God to do something which otherwise He would not do. Of course it does not compel God by any magic force, but it moves Him as one man by his request moves another.*

More recently, Günther Bornkamm elaborated:

Jesus speaks of prayer in this "unholy" way so as to dispel the mist of "pious" thought which has always surrounded prayer: in mysticism, which understands it as an exercise for purification and contemplation; in the piety of the Stoics, in which its only function is to become one in praise with the providence of God; in Jewish thought, where prayer is part of the works of the pious. The "fatherhood" of God means what it says. We can therefore not speak of him in a human enough way, if he is not to be removed to a distant nebulous sanctity and become a mere spectre. Jesus' teaching about prayer is the proclamation of the nearness of God.†

For secular Christians, Jesus' winsome, childlike understanding exacerbates the problems of belief beyond the capacity easily to manage. They know that man lives in a universe unimaginably large and old, according to all present evidence on the only planet in the totality of that universe upon which there is human life (only statistical probabilities keep alive the flickering hope that man is not alone in the cosmos). They are asked to believe that the sovereign power governing such an immense impersonal order has chosen human beings on this obscure planet to

* Rudolf Bultmann, *Jesus and the Word* (New York: Charles Scribner's Sons, 1934), pp. 184-85.
† Günther Bornkamm, *Jesus of Nazareth* (New York: Harper & Brothers, 1961), p. 135.

15

be "little lower than the angels" and has deemed all things important to the degree that they contribute to these pitiable creatures' welfare. It is much easier to believe long-discredited alternatives to biblical faith than it is to recover the lost perspective of childhood, apparently so vital in Jesus' faith. For example, one could posit more plausibly that at the creation God imposed a fixed order on things which not even he will modify, and that he now remains utterly apart from his creation, a silent, impassive observer of the whole, marveling in its intricate design but heedless of petitions from within. Or, if deism seems fraught with insuperable difficulties in its own right, the accommodation between faith and secularity might be attempted by appealing to the classical doctrine of divine transcendence: One could suppose that God's very holiness precludes that he could ever submit to the crude and worldly requests of men; he must remain eternally unavailable. In both views, belief in God is thoroughly compatible with the absence of divinely wrought effects in experience. Neither view of the God-world relationship is mere speculation on man's part; both have firm support in tradition. Thus, it is tempting to affirm something like one of these alternatives and quietly blur Jesus' distinctive words of address to "Abba, Father." Such faith expressed an intimacy of communion presumptuous to the point of scandal in Jesus' own day and wholly incredible to many in the contemporary world.

Even if, somehow, one could come to believe with Jesus in the possibility of a God both holy and accessible, he would then confront the most awesome difficulty of all. God frequently does fulfill human requests. But there is no obvious pattern in his gracious apportioning of benefits to the actualities of human need. Can man, then, speak truly of trusting in God's benevolence? Who does not know of desperate circumstances which remained unrelieved, even though earnest believers prayed incessantly?

For every miracle wrought in answer to prayer, there are seemingly a hundred instances of failure on God's part to respond as he had been asked, a hundred silences to heartfelt and heartsick petitions. Does God then mock his creatures by promising that they have only to ask in order to receive? Does faith reduce to trusting in God's wisdom to dispose of man's petitions in ways wholly beyond human comprehension?

It cannot be overlooked, then, how radically Jesus' faith calls into question contemporary man's most persuasive convictions about himself and his world. While Jesus understands God in the traditional manner as the source and sustainer of all things, who knows and is present in all things, what is most important about Jesus' faith is his unconquerable trust that God comes to and abides with every human being in ways uniquely appropriate to each. For Jesus, God's ways of remaining present are infinitely variegated, always adapted to the infinite diversities of his creatures. Sustainer of all things, in his infinite capacity to be present God nevertheless is able to pause indefinitely with each creature; sovereign over all, he is never far from any. No human governor is, has been, or can ever be capable of harmonizing both personally and efficiently the lives of all other human beings and the human environing world as such (or even an infinitesimal portion thereof). Man's powers of remaining caringly present and yet effectively sustaining those cared for are drastically limited; his blundering efforts to create a humane environment and his incapacity for intimacy with more than a few other human beings display his finitude starkly. But over human creative agency, secular man is asked to believe, there is One whose power of sustaining presence, relationship, and authority is infinite. Is it any wonder that for contemporary man the power of prayer seems so ineffectual? Everything about Jesus' God seems to collide with worldly wisdom about what God could

17

be like, if there were such. It is irrelevant to seek consolation in the Pauline view that God appears foolish only to those worldly creatures who are perishing by their specious wisdom. For there is nothing in the apostle's view of the "wisdom of God" which would lend support to the view that, in the light of that wisdom, all worldly understanding is annulled.

GOD AND SECULAR BELIEF

Clearly, the possibility of prayer of the sort in which Jesus engaged depends wholly upon the possibility of a vital faith in God. Yet at no time in the history of Christianity has the possibility of belief in God, whether on Jesus' terms or any other, become dubious to so many as in the contemporary era. Though discourse about God has always been difficult (in different ways for the believer than for the unbeliever), until recently it has been regarded as at least a respectable deployment of interest even by those who were not themselves willing to engage in earnest. At present, however, there persists pervasive doubt that any language (faith language or otherwise) in which the term God appears can make sense at all. What is now in question is not the truth of Christian belief about God but rather the possibility of articulating an intelligible claim about God which could even be *considered* worthy of assent. Contemporary philosophical and theological inquiries suggest at least five interrelated reasons why belief in God has assumed such questionable status.

1. *It has come to be appreciated anew that the God concept is the indispensable foundation for any and all Christian discourse.* Much innovative theology since the early nineteenth century sought to interpret Christian faith by means of concepts derived either from an examination of the person of Jesus Christ or from Enlightenment-

inspired theories of human nature, rather than beginning, as one would have expected, with an exposition of the existence and nature of God. While the reasons for these interesting experiments are too complex to be explored here, at least a few brief statements about the substance of the resulting programs are in order.

Friedrich Schleiermacher's theology affirmed the centrality of Jesus as the basis of Christianity's unique understanding of God; in *The Christian Faith*, his comprehensive work in dogmatics, all speech about God virtually reduces to statements about Jesus of Nazareth. Many important theologians followed Schleiermacher on this point: Kierkegaard, Ritschl, Harnack, Hermann, Barth, and Brunner, to cite only a few. The diverse possibilities inherent in such a program can be illustrated by noting the different ways Schleiermacher and Barth emphasized Jesus' centrality for a doctrine of God: Schleiermacher's Christology focuses upon Jesus' self-consciousness while Barth's concentrates upon the Word of which Jesus is the embodiment. Still another direction was suggested by this same theological program, for Schleiermacher also insisted with uncompromising rigor that all significant statements about God depend upon some prior and defensible account of the conditions under which God can be humanly apprehended. Upon this view, a theory of human understanding, and to this extent therefore a doctrine of man, is both the necessary preface to and the substance of theology; what can be said about God is determined by the human cognitive structure through which alone revelation is appropriated. An inverted form of Hegel's philosophy permitted Feuerbach to draw this same conclusion: Theology is anthropology. Though only Feuerbach denied that in the religious consciousness a being other than man, God, appears, every theologian standing in this tradition would have maintained that images of God illumine man

19

the image-maker more adequately than they express the truth about God.

Recently, however, serious attempts to change the direction of these trends are in evidence, all of which arise out of a twofold realization: (a) that there can be no distinctively Christian anthropology apart from reference to Jesus Christ as the normative expression of full humanness and (b) that Jesus himself is incomprehensible apart from his all-consuming faith in God. The apostolic witness to Jesus' faith is unequivocal on the latter point especially; to doubt the foundational significance to his life and ministry of his belief in God is to deny the authoritativeness of the entire New Testament record. The person of Christ is important for faith only insofar as and because it achieves transparency to the God in whom Jesus believed. Though Jesus Christ may indeed be the only begotten Son of the Father, who alone truly reveals the Father, it is to that Father and not to himself that his saving work points. Thus, if Christians' loyalties really are to that concrete historical individual whose being was given over to obedient service to God, they must place "God" at the very center of their speech and lives. The "new quest" for the historical Jesus should have made plain to everyone that Jesus was, above all, a "God-intoxicated man." It is strange, then, that theologians, especially of German vintage, continue to mine the played-out christological and anthropological terrain: Moltmann and Pannenberg the former and the Bultmannians the latter. By contrast, in the English-speaking theological world the problem of God has come to be the focus increasingly: in England, in the aftermath of the "Honest to God" discussion, and in America as a response to the popularity of the radical theologians, alternatives to which include especially the work of Schubert Ogden, Robert Neville, and Gordon Kaufman. What probably accounts for the Anglo-Saxon character of this *theo*logical revival is the fact that the decisive questions about the possibility of any speech about God come from a philosophical perspective which English-speaking philosophers and theologians embraced with greater and more enduring vigor than did their German colleagues: positivism and its more recent expressions in linguistic philosophy. To those influenced by this latter philosophical program, it cannot suffice to employ christological or anthropological symbols as the basis for a doctrine of God if on independent grounds it appears that any speech about God is of dubious intelligibility. Confronting this charge directly involves supposing at the outset the primacy of the God question for all serious theologizing.

If belief in God is no longer possible for contemporary man, Jesus cannot remain a suitable focus for human commitment. No human being can be the ideal for humanity and yet be fundamentally in error about the very thing that matters to him most. By way of illustration, it is instructive to note that liberal theology failed to persuade many that Jesus could be mankind's exemplar even if he were mistaken about the coming of the final judgment. Given the importance of the idea of an immanent end of human history in Jesus' own self-understanding, it is difficult, if not impossible, to take him seriously for very long if it must be admitted that his understanding of the end time was egregiously in error. The scandal of the gospel for a secular age is not that Jesus was born of a woman, that he forgave sins, died on a cross, or that he was raised from the dead; it must be simply that he believed with his whole being in God.

2. *Speech about God has come to refer increasingly to events obscured in an irretrievable past.* Contemporary theology has pursued relentlessly but without happy issue the *present* reality of God, striving mightily to answer Lessing's question of how the ugly, widening ditch separating the present from the past can be traversed, how recollection can make possible the appropriation in the

21

present of God's historic revelation. The chief result of these labors is a new concept of revelation as God's *self*-disclosure in the present, in whose power the reliability of past testimony is somehow authenticated. Neo-orthodoxy and mysticism converge as each in its own way stresses the present experience of divine reality; one seeks to express the divine presence in language that is both fitting and communicative while the other basks in ecstatic rapture of the ineffable. Neither is content with the classical view of revelation as an imparting of information, transmitted from past to present through tradition, largely because upon such an understanding the contemporary believer could stand only in an indirect relationship with God; in Kierkegaard's term, he would be a disciple only at second hand.

In both, however, preoccupation with the present is really a forced option, precisely because it is no longer possible to believe without qualification that past revelation is accessible to memory. Until at least the time of the Enlightenment, the church's faith was solidly anchored in commemoration of an authoritative past mediated by scripture and tradition. In their being remembered, it could be held, historic moments repeated themselves: to re-present and celebrate the mighty acts of God in the past was to participate in their salvific power for the present. But since the Enlightenment every attempt to define the contours of faith by reference to a holy history has encountered numerous shattering difficulties, all proceeding from growing doubts about the reliability of the witness mediated through the tradition. Prior to the Enlightenment one could feel certain that divine inspiration, of the Bible and in the church, ensures the trustworthiness of the traditions upon which subsequent generations of believers are dependent. But once that tradition is scrutinized according to procedures widely acknowledged as appropriate for ascertaining the reliability of any and all accounts of the past, belief in the sufficiency of scripture and tradition becomes increasingly problematic, for several reasons.

In the first place, it has come to be seen that the earliest manuscripts available of the canonical scriptures, upon which the church's tradition depends, are considerably later in composition than the events to which they refer, by 150 years in the case of even isolated fragments of the New Testament. As for a complete text of the New Testament, the earliest presently available date from the fourth century. Secondly, all extant manuscripts reflect creative editing throughout, the imposition of interpretation upon collections of earlier strands of both oral and written tradition of diverse and in many cases unknown origin. This observation is crucial with respect to the Gospels, since it is these documents which ground the distinctive character of the early church's kerygma in the life and ministry of Jesus; the Pauline corpus and various materials from Acts cannot by themselves constitute the requisite authority upon which the church bases its proclamation of the Lordship of Christ. While one cannot but admire the theological sensitivity and literary skill of the Gospel writers, that their work synthesizes materials of widely differing forms which reflect considerably varied historical situations must call into question any naïve supposition that they render a sufficiently clear and detailed narration of revelatory events in the past to serve as *the* wellspring of faith for all time.

Though it may be possible to dismantle the manuscripts available into their original components, even when such form-critical work is done at a very high level it remains debatable in the extreme whether any of the resulting "units" provides sufficiently comprehensive testimony from the disciples' own time. Even if it could be said that some of their contents are from Jesus himself, they cannot be assembled in such a way as to provide anything like a detailed chronology of Jesus' life. It is convenient to say that one ought not be concerned about a life of Jesus when such a life cannot be written. But if the New Testament's account of God's decisive self-revelation is to be understood as focused from beginning to end upon the person of Jesus, it *must* provide the data for a detailed chronology of Jesus' life, because only through such could there be exhibited the developmental process through which Jesus gradually came to his unique mission. What is most important about God's revelation in Jesus Christ is the way in which it came to incarnation in a wholly human form. To suppose divine revelation to have been complete from the very moment of Jesus' conception or birth, and not to undergo cumulative development, is to obscure the whole point of the doctrine of the Incarnate Lord: that human life, intrinsically developmental, is an appropriate vehicle for God's own being. From this perspective, it is a grave deficiency that the materials from the time of Jesus do not shed sufficient light on the fundamental question of Jesus' own self-understanding. Why, for example, did he turn toward Jerusalem at the crucial time in his ministry and what did he expect to transpire there? It is quite conceivable that Jesus had no clear idea, upon entering Jerusalem, what the outcome of the week would be; he may have supposed that upon his entrance the "last days" would be brought to completion with the dramatic ushering in of the promised Kingdom of God. If this conjecture is borne out in fact, then Jesus' presumed authoritative witness to the divine will becomes radically questionable.

All of these difficulties are accentuated greatly when consideration is given to revelation in the Old Testament. Many centuries separate the written account from the exodus event to which Old Testament faith bears witness (and, not altogether facetiously, one might note that even more centuries separate the extant written accounts from the creation of the world). The conclusion which seems to follow is that though God may have revealed himself in the past, that past is no longer specifiable with sufficient clarity to provide communal memory with a determining focus historically well grounded. What is preserved is the remembrance of a people's belief about God, but not the reality to which their beliefs refer and the events out of which they may have arisen. While the church's memories may continue to constitute the *occasion* for believing, it is becoming increasingly doubtful that they ought to comprise the *substance* of believing. Unless the God in whom one believes, through the memories, is experienceable also independently of those memories, the memories themselves lose much of their former authoritativeness.

It is the underlying conviction in Christian circles, theologies of secularity and hope to the contrary notwithstanding, that revelatory events are primarily in the past. This is evident from the fact that it is almost universally taken for granted that divine impingement in the present cannot be discerned at all except as man's understanding is guided by a framework of interpretation itself authorized by virtue of its adequacy to past revelations. Roman Catholicism steadfastly refuses, even since Vatican Council II, to understand dogma as evolving; whatever dogma expresses, it comes from the past and contains already all its possible interpretations which will ensue through the centuries. And Protestants continue to act as if the canon of scripture were closed, as if with the writing of Revelation (or perhaps 2 Peter) no fresh disclosures of God have occurred. By way of a final example, modernist Christians often concede that miracles may have occurred once upon a time, but no longer. In sum, then, if God's revelation is given in a series of past occurrences (*Heilsgeschichte*) which also and alone provide the norms and criteria for determining whether revelation has occurred again in the present, that it cannot readily be specified what those past occurrences are may come to constitute a fatal deficiency in any and all speech about God.

3. *Speech about God no longer enhances man's understanding of the world.* For some time, it has been conceded widely that belief in God yields no *explanation* of the world in which man lives: As Laplace stated to Napoleon, researchers have no need for such a hypothesis. There is nothing especially profound about this observation; it is doubtful that belief in God ever functioned for religious people primarily as a way of explaining anything. What is important, however, is the suggestion that speech about divine realities is no longer that by and through which human beings achieve orientation in the experienced orders of nature and history; transcendent references no longer have illuminative power for mundane and profane human existence (i.e., in the saeculum). References to God by secular-minded people seem increasingly artificial. For example, though from time to time even secular Christians may utter sincerely prayers of adoration and submission, few would dream of seeking to manipulate nature's uniform sequences by means of petitionary or intercessory prayer. When all hope is lost, the unabashedly contemporary man, and even the atheist, may pray for a remission of leukemia, but *only* when all hope is lost is he likely to *think* to do so. How one comes to grips with a world which includes the possibility that he will become a leukemia victim, or that he and his kind will be cremated in a humanly engineered atomic holocaust, is less and less regulated by his convictions about transcendent realities. Few any longer proffer the traditional belief that "God is testing man's faith" as an illuminating insight into the tragic ways of the world. And it is no longer convincing to dismiss such skepticism by simply noting that its unbelieving posture obviates the necessity that any believer should take it seriously. Increasingly, secularity is presupposed in every conception of faith; believers are

coming to understand accepting responsibility for their world themselves through their own powers of valuing and choosing.

The works of Friedrich Gogarten and the later Dietrich Bonhoeffer represent brilliant attempts to baptize in the name of faith secular man's belief that he alone must assume the burden of fashioning his world. Each theologian, in his own way, maintained that it is God's own desire that men function in this creative, self-regulating, and responsible manner. But their endeavors to translate into thoroughly secular terms human speech about God are singularly unconvincing. To insist that references to God are especially meaningful to those who constitute their own worlds in freedom and responsibility, that God has absented himself in order that his creatures can orient themselves creatively apart from God, is to presuppose rather than to confer intelligibility upon the God concept, a maneuver the appropriateness of which is precisely the issue in question. For why should one who can function in a world from which God is absent feel any obligation whatsoever to continue living as if there were *no* God while affirming with assurance that, after all, there *is*? How could one choose to live as if it is God's design that there appears to be no God? Is there any significant difference between believing that there is a God who acts as if there were not, and not believing that there is a God at all? It cannot be religiously significant to think of God as the transcendent "It" of a cosmic hide-and-seek game. Faith is committed to the proposition that believing in God is positively enhancing to life; the theologian must elucidate the experiential basis of that belief in such a manner that human beings can see clearly how faith uniquely exhibits the fullest potentialities of human existence, horizons which secular life does not, and perhaps cannot, envision. To celebrate merely going about one's business freely though responsibly, and thereby to evade

27

the crucial questions about man's constitutive relationship to *transcendent* reality, is to lose sight of faith itself in the glare of secular achievements.

4. *Speech about God appears not to conform to the conditions for informative speech generally.* According to generally agreed-upon criteria for "cognitive meaningfulness," sentences in which the word God is the subject, believers' intentions to the contrary notwithstanding, cannot express anything about the real nature of things; they do not assume the form of statements which could be said and shown to be true or false. The contemporary philosophical doctrine of cognitive meaningfulness upon which this so-called consensus rests can be stated as follows: (a) A cognitively meaningful expression is one which asserts that something is the case (it expresses a matter of fact), (b) To express that something is the case is at once to deny that its opposite is the case (A ≡ not not-A), (c) Hence, for any claim to be cognitively meaningful, the opposite of that claim must be conceivable: one must be able to conceive the opposite in order to express it as a denial of the original claim (it may also be the case that for any expression to be cognitively meaningful, its opposite must be both conceivable and conceivable as true, (d) Finally, from (c) it follows that for any expression to be cognitively meaningful, some state of affairs under which its opposite might be true must also be conceivable.

The thrust of the doctrine as a whole is that for any truth claim it must be possible to envision circumstances which, if occurring, would falsify that claim by entailing the truth of a claim opposite to it. The crucial point is that not only must the opposite of a claim be conceivable for that claim to be cognitively meaningful, the occurrences which would entail its opposite must also be conceivable. For example, if "The planet earth sustains human life" is a cognitively meaningful claim, it must be possible, first, to conceive without contradiction some proposition expressing its denial: "The earth may not sustain human life." More importantly still, conditions implying the latter also must be conceivable without contradiction: a change, for example, in the earth's atmosphere to a methane base. A true proposition expressing the fact of such a change would entail the denial of the original proposition.

Though exhibiting a complex development with many variants among contemporary philosophers, this elusive doctrine of cognitive meaningfulness functions in contemporary philosophical discourse almost as a dogma, in spite of many difficulties accompanying it. As stated, the doctrine calls seriously into question the intelligibility of faith's truth claims about God at points (c) and (d). No one seriously denies that believers intend to assert something, and by doing so to deny other assertions, such as Freud's that God is an illusion: (a) and (b) above. But in reference to points (c) and (d) of this doctrine, serious questions begin to arise. With regard to (c), since the time of Anselm it has been a major emphasis among many theologians that no denial of God's existence can make sense; only the fool says in his heart, "There is no God." The function of the so-called ontological argument for the existence of God, as Anselm conceived it, is to point up the strange logical features of the concept of God, the most important of which is that, unlike other truth claims, statements in which this concept functions cannot have significant denials; a supremely perfect being cannot be conceived not to exist. From the inconceivability of its contrary, some theologians have argued, the statement "God exists" is shown to be not merely true but necessarily true.

On point (d), if the Christian doctrine of creation is taken seriously, which affirms among other things that by the term God is meant the source of all there is, the word God becomes the name of a being (or of Being-as-such) compatible with any and all conditions; hence, true statements about God would seem to be implied by every true statement about anything, as statements about any effect imply further statements about its cause. To say the least, this is an odd characteristic for any being to possess. Ordinarily, one is inclined to believe that much of what any being does matters and can matter to no other being; part of the career of each being is wholly interior to itself, without import or implication for any other being. Speech about God, on the contrary, supposes a being to whom every other being matters and who is implied by every other being whatever. No finite being is implied by *every* other being; each finite being is compatible with only *some* other finite beings. Thus, no finite being abides no matter what. "God," however, is the name of a being subject to no conditions whatever, who persists through every set of circumstances and is signified, to the sufficiently discerning at least, by every set of circumstances. Frequently, contingencies such as adversity weaken the intensity of *believing*, but one who understands Christian belief in God knows that the wax and wane of commitment has no bearing upon the *reality* of that to which one is supposed to remain committed. For example, nothing that happened to Job could have the slightest relevance for the truth or falsity of his belief in God, except perhaps that what happened to him must be regarded as somehow entailing the truth of that belief. The peculiar logic of Christian utterances about God is that they claim for themselves a form of license not ordinarily granted to speech about any other thing. By doing so, according to the philosophical doctrine previously elaborated, their fundamental term, God, can express no determinate subject matter at all upon which to reflect. If they are relevant to everything, assertions about God could not express anything (a proposition which expresses everything expresses no-thing). Christian speech about God seems to suffer the demise of utter abstraction.

5. *Speech about God seems to express only the wishful hope that reality will uphold the most worthwhile strivings of human existence.* The similarities between images of God in religious literature and those of sheer fantasy give rise to the haunting suggestion that belief in God may be merely a creative work of man's imagination, a wordplay which dabs upon the data of experience the objectification of human fancy only. For example:

The man and his wife heard the sound of the Lord God walking in the garden at the time of the evening breeze and hid from the Lord God among the trees of the garden. But the Lord God called to the man and said to him, 'Where are you?'
—Genesis 3:8-9, NEB

When Moses entered it, the pillar of cloud came down, and stayed at the entrance to the tent while the Lord spoke with Moses. As soon as the people saw the pillar of cloud standing at the entrance to the tent, they would all prostrate themselves, every man at the entrance to his tent. The Lord would speak with Moses face to face, as one man speaks to another.
—Exodus 33:9-11a, NEB

When Israel was a child, I loved him,
    and out of Egypt I called my son.
The more I called them,
    the more they went from me;
they kept sacrificing to the Ba'als,
    and burning incense to idols.

Yet it was I who taught E'phraim to walk,
    I took them up in my arms;
    but they did not know that I healed them.
I led them with cords of compassion,

31

with the bands of love,
and I became to them as one
    who eases the yoke on their jaws,
    and I bent down to them and fed them.

They shall return to the land of Egypt,
    and Assyria shall be their king,
    because they have refused to return to me.
The sword shall rage against their cities,
    consume the bars of their gates,
    and devour them in their fortresses.
My people are bent on turning away from me;
    so they are appointed to the yoke,
    and none shall remove it.

How can I give you up, O E'phraim!
    How can I hand you over, O Israel!
How can I make you like Admah!
    How can I treat you like Zeboi'im!
My heart recoils within me,
    my compassion grows warm and tender.
I will not execute my fierce anger,
    I will not again destroy E'phraim;
for I am God and not man,
    the Holy One in your midst,
    and I will not come to destroy.
                    —Hosea 11:1-9

Perhaps it was imagery such as this which first provoked
Feuerbach to consider that man's idea of God results from
an act of self-deception. For Feuerbach, man projects the
form of a being other than himself from preconceived
ideas of what Ideal Humanity should be like; God is
merely a name for the human race's outermost possibilities. Freud believed he had discovered that religious belief arises out of the illusions man creates to make less

intimidating his mandatory passage from infantile to civilized existence; the biological parent who nurtures his every whim in infancy reappears "behind" the cosmos to support him when he strikes out on his own.

Theologians always have seemed to feel that the anthropomorphism of faith language is a burden which must be overcome by a combination of rigorous thinking about and deepening devotion to a God posited as Wholly Other. As popular piety always betrays, however, neither has been notably successful in purging language about God of its altogether human imagery and conceptuality. No matter how threatening the charge of blasphemy is made, men of faith stubbornly persist in affirming a God who is *a* being and not Being-itself, and a being very much like themselves in both appearance and nature at that. As will be shown later, Christian language cannot represent its users at all apart from just such anthropomorphic vocabulary at its foundation, unless it abandons entirely its moorings in scripture and tradition; though theology may demythologize traditional faith language, it cannot deanthropomorphize it. Christian faith cannot evade the challenge that its beliefs are mere "make-believe," the result of hypostatizing what men long for but never experience directly. Christianity is irrevocably committed to the view that everything conspires to uphold human judgments about what is good and true and beautiful, that all that is harmonizes with what human beings believe to be harmonious in their most discerning acts of judgment.

Such presumption clearly borders on the preposterous, for a close look at the natural order discloses an immensity which renders insignificant life on this planet. Even if statistically it is highly probable that man is not alone in the universe, it remains painfully evident that things generally resemble more the nonliving than the living. To be sure, in recent times the natural order has come to be regarded more as a nexus of human possibility than as a given which is impervious to those conscious beings who gaze upon it. And contemporary forms of humanism affirm boldly the primacy of man as the determiner both of the order of being and of the order of value, as if things neither are, nor are good, unless they are pertinent in some way to human reality. Since both ways of looking at things seem shot through with the same anthropomorphism descried in religious matters, it might appear strange that the gross anthropomorphism of Christian language should constitute such a stumbling block to secular-minded believers nowadays. However, although humanism may be naïve about the place of man in the universe, that cannot constitute a justification for any similar naïveté on the part of Christian believers. To suppose for a moment that this "terrestrial ball" is sustained in its course by a being like man is to sink into the abyss of childhood fantasy unless careful and cogent argumentation can be brought to the supposition's defense.

In sum, there is at least a fivefold problematic connected with any and all such speech about God, and especially with the kind of belief in God which characterizes the faith of Jesus. Unless by close analysis of the whole the force of each problem can be minimized, it must be questioned seriously whether it is possible to speak any longer in traditional ways about God. As secular man confronts the possibility of prayer, what he can bring himself to believe and do will remain conditioned and possibly determined by these considerations. These difficulties must be overcome, or at least minimized, if prayer is to be possible for believers who also are participants in a secular world.

Preliminary to dealing with these foundational issues directly, an attempt will be made to develop a systematic account of the phenomenon of prayer itself. The chapter immediately following will elaborate upon the *context, formal structure*, and *inner dynamics* of prayer. Following a depiction of the actuality of prayer, the focus will shift to a more detailed consideration of the conditions which make prayer a significant possibility: the belief structure presupposed by and implied in prayer. At this juncture, the impact of secular consciousness will begin to appear explicitly, setting the agenda of topics for the concluding chapter.

1751128

CHAPTER 2

THE EXPERIENCE
OF PRAYER

The purpose of this chapter is to offer one understanding of prayer as it is actually engaged in by believers, in order that the peculiar impingement which secular consciousness makes upon the possibility of prayer can be confronted fully and in depth. It will not suffice to minimize the challenges by means of an approach which takes neither secularity nor the phenomenon of prayer seriously: for example, by caricaturing the secular attitude as one of godless materialism with which no good Christian should have anything to do, or by misinterpreting prayer as merely a meditative process which facilitates understanding of and adjustment to a fixed order of reality. Both attempts will enable one to overcome the force of the prayer-secularity problem, but at the expense of the conflicting modes of experience all of which secular believers desire to celebrate. What follows is an attempt to present the Christian practice of prayer in a way which takes both the received tradition and contemporary understanding as normative for all believers. The analysis seeks to lay bare both the living reality and the problematic of prayer.

PRAYER AND COMMUNITY

Clearly, there are distinctions to be made between the language of prayer and prayer-like language used for other than prayerful purposes. For example, the expression "Lord have mercy on us" can arise both at a high point of formal ritual and over a floor cluttered with the groceries whose sack proved less than capable of fulfilling the demands placed upon it. This latter utterance cannot be understood as an act of faith. Nor can language be prayerful which importunes the Deity to place a curse upon especially irritating objects, such as the hammer which has just smashed a thumb. Through what prior understanding of prayer is this distinction understood by all?

Presumably, through an understanding of prayer as an act of faith which arises out of life shared in a community of believers, one response to the divine initiative which calls faith itself into being. Through prayer, believers direct their attention to the whole response of faith required by God and by so doing prepare themselves for engaging in its every expression (belief, trust, worship, service, sacrifice) with deepening understanding of why such a life of faith is appropriate. Because there is a meditative as well as a dialogue side to prayer, a thinking-about as well as a conversing-with God, prayer is an especially profound way for an individual to acknowledge and embody the impingement of that Other which transcends every other claim upon his loyalty. Fundamentally, however, prayer remains faithful address to the One who has made a *community's* faith possible.

The assertion that prayer is an act of faith may seem to be contradicted by innumerable instances of prayers which human beings actually and frequently do offer. Frequently, prayers are uttered seemingly in earnest which do not in any obvious way arise out of communal faith, prayers which really exclaim unfaith, prayers *for* and not *in* faith, desperate cries for God in extreme situations when life itself is at stake. "In the foxhole (or on the launching pad) there are no atheists." Even though the

37

threatened individual may have been conspicuously devoid of religious commitment throughout his life, when that life hangs in the balance, any prayerful cry he utters usually is considered without question to be a genuinely prayerful act. In the hospital room of a dying child, whose agonies are too much both for the child and for the parents to bear, only prayer may seem to suffice, and it seems not to matter whether it is offered by creatures of faith or unfaith. In extremis, the right to pray seems unconditioned by the quality of one's participation in a community of belief. Nevertheless, though it would be unseemly in such situations to question explicitly an unbeliever's intention to pray, it is misleading to suppose that just these kinds of situations exhibit the real nature of prayer. However existentially serious it may be, a hopeless plea in intolerable circumstances for God-alone-knows-what, by individuals for whom faith is merely a last resort, cannot constitute genuine prayer.

It cannot be denied that both prayer and faith become possible for many only in boundary situations, but that in some of those situations prayer can and does articulate a plea in the absence of faith for the very realities to which faith bears witness. Mere cries of desperation, grief, or shock ("Oh, my God!"), however, are exclamatory utterances only, whose sole function is to conduct the charge of the feelings which give rise to them. However genuinely they may be provoked by unfortunate circumstances, they cannot meaningfully be said to constitute prayers because they are not consciously addressed to a caring Being whose existence is already presumed to be at least a serious possibility for belief. Really to pray is to be persuaded, however tentatively and for whatever reason, of the possibility that in and beyond the perceived world there exists an omnipresent Being capable of hearing and responding effectively to human address. This is not to say that really to pray, a given individual must self-consciously participate in some circle of faith. It is to say, however, that his self-understanding cannot wholly preclude such participation, his denials to the contrary notwithstanding. He cannot have ruled out the possibility of faith-in-community, or else his crisis prayers would make no sense at all, other than as expressions only of his sense of hopelessness.

> Be merciful to me, O Lord, for I am weak;
> heal me, my very bones are shaken;
> my soul quivers in dismay.
> And thou, O Lord—how long?
> Come back, O Lord; set my soul free,
> deliver me for thy love's sake.
> None talk of thee among the dead;
> who praises thee in Sheol?
>
> I am wearied with groaning;
> all night long my pillow is wet with tears,
> I soak my bed with weeping.
> Grief dims my eyes;
> they are worn out with all my woes.
> —Psalm 6:2-7, NEB

For some, bare possibility is the only status that faith ever assumes. Even among believers, doubt and insecurity about faith persist in their responses to the world; the most intense believers sometimes discover that faith is no longer the vital and governing reality in life. Genuine faith has doubt within it as an ever-present possibility. Especially within the company of the faithful, the life of faith is a continuing and agonizing struggle between belief and unbelief, whose outcome may never be certain at any stage along the believer's way. Throughout the struggle, however, the minimal conviction abides that faith *is* a possibility, no matter how remote a possibility it may be at any given moment, that doing some faithful thing, however low the level of intensity may be which accompanies the doing, makes some sense. What this suggests is that no one can long for faith if he has not already in some sense experienced the presence of that Other who calls faith into being and sustains its development. Instead of referring to certain prayers as prayers *for* faith, therefore, it would be more accurate to deem them prayers which reflect a rudimentary response of faith petitioning for a more profound revelation: "Lord, I believe; help my unbelief." To someone utterly outside the circle of faith, for whom faith cannot constitute even a possibility, such a language must appear utterly contradictory. But believers know the logic of it. For both the self-conscious believer and the one who has never considered himself such but now in a crisis finds himself praying, faith is never over against nonfaith; it is an imperfect and incomplete faith grasping for integrity and wholeness of expression.

There is still another view of prayer which seems to contradict the thesis that the believing community comprises the locus for genuine prayer. For some, prayer is merely one way of articulating the natural striving of religious man (*homo religiosus*) toward transcendent reality, an urge which expresses itself independently of involvements in the activities of specific religious communities. Upon this view, the reality to which religious yearning points is considered to be more profound than that which "the churches" could ever grasp; it is understood as a transcendent dimension utterly beyond the outer limits of human possibility, upon which, however, all human possibilities converge. Prayer expresses the universal desire to meditate upon what is in itself wholly indeterminate but which is manifest as a lure to human intellect, will, and desire, making its impact independently from the influences of concrete religious histories and

40

institutions upon human self-consciousness and development. To these claims, two replies are cogent.

In the first place, longing for Transcendent Reality-as-such is generated at all only by some concrete impingement of that Reality upon some particular inquirer. Whatever may remain unfathomable about Transcendence, every image and concept of it presupposes its having encountered individuals in highly specific ways; every description of the encounters will bear inescapably the marks of the recipients' own vantage points in time along with the disclosure of the Ultimate in itself. To put the point in the language of finite and infinite, finite creatures cannot even yearn for the Infinite unless the Infinite is already present to the finite self in finitely appropriable ways. Secondly, the means (i.e., images, concepts, utterances, etc.) by which men express Transcendent Reality arise out of some particular religious tradition and derive their significance wholly from the development of that tradition: i.e., "Behold, the Lamb of God, who takes away the sin of the world (John 1:29)." In the specific tradition upon which one depends, what transcends may be perceived only dimly. But only as embodied in specific traditions can the Transcendent be perceived at all; some particular faithful community is presupposed even in the most universalist-sounding prayers which aspire to a cogency beyond the circumscribed possibilities of limited human communities. Prayers exhibit with peculiar clarity that the responses of those who consciously experience the impingements of Transcendent Reality are dependent upon the availability of concrete images and concepts rooted in a historically identifiable community. Prayers of address to the Transcendent are vital only when the Transcendent is conceived specifically by those means already invested with meaning by the community: i.e., Yahweh, Allah, Krishna, etc.

41

With regard to Christian prayer specifically, John 17 teaches that the Christian prays because he has already been touched by *Jesus Christ's* intercession on his behalf before God, making access to God possible; through that intercession, God forgives men of their sins and promises in love to be with the believer continually:

Holy Father, keep them in thy name, which thou hast given me. . . . I do not pray for these only, but also for those who believe in me through their word, that they may all be one; even as thou, Father, art in me, and I in thee, that they also may be in us, so that the world may believe that thou hast sent me. The glory which thou hast given me I have given to them, that they may be one even as we are one, I in them and thou in me, that they may become perfectly one, so that the world may know that thou hast sent me and hast loved them even as thou hast loved me. Father, I desire that they also, whom thou hast given me, may be with me where I am, to behold my glory which thou hast given me in thy love for me before the foundation of the world.

—John 17:11b, 20-24

At Romans 8:26-27 (NEB), the apostle Paul writes that the Christian prays because he has experienced the power of the *Spirit* interceding for him before God, whose power alone enables him to pray:

In the same way the Spirit comes to the aid of our weakness. We do not even know how we ought to pray, but through our inarticulate groans the Spirit himself is pleading for us, and God who searches our inmost being knows what the Spirit means, because he pleads for God's people in God's own way.

According to both these passages, prayer is to be understood as one way of affirming through one's life-style the claims of a specific community's understanding about transcendent realities which are comprehensible only as embodied in *some* community's historic witness. The symbols "Jesus the Christ" and "Spirit of God," themselves meaningful only to those who stand historically within the Judeo-Christian tradition, wholly determine the believer's understanding of what he is about when he truly prays to the God and Father of his Lord Jesus Christ.

Second, from the standpoint of Christian nurture, prayer is an instructive sign of and clue to the intensity and quality of a believer's faith. To put the point negatively, the absence or diminishment of prayer is an indication that one's faith may be in difficulty, albeit for any number of reasons. While it may seem presumptuous to propose that prayer may function as a criterion for assessing the quality of faith, more specifically for measuring growth in faith, Calvin's insight into the importance of prayer suggests the appropriateness of so regarding it: In Calvin's thinking Christians who do not pray are in fact practicing *blasphemy* in that they are ignoring God's own promises. Every religious community needs some such criteria if its adherents truly are to become priests to their brothers, calling one another to come to terms with themselves, even and especially through serious criticism. What makes criticism bearable and helpful is its offer within a community of love by individuals who also are willing to open themselves to the same testing by a brother.

In addition to its normally communal setting, the examination of faith by reference to the condition of prayer life also can be conducted introspectively; one can determine in part the faithfulness of his own life by looking honestly at the kind of faith which seems to be emergent (or not) in his private prayers. Thus, there is all the more reason to strive for utmost clarity about the nature of prayer when by doing so one may come to have at hand a readily applicable standard by which to examine the adequacy of one's entire life of faith. To take stock of oneself and others as believers, in the light of a clear understanding of what prayer in general ought to be and how one's own prayers do and do not exhibit the fullness of prayer, is one cogent way to carry out the biblical injunction to "test the spirits [at work within men] to see whether they are of God (1 John 4:1)." Though it may be difficult to assess another's faith by observing his personal prayer life, it surely is possible to understand oneself thusly.

Theologians especially need to preoccupy themselves with the actualities of the life of prayer, since prayer expresses the heart of a believer's faith and since it is their primary task to clarify faith understandingly. As theology seeks primarily to understand rather than to provoke or negate faith, then prayer well may be the most important subject matter with which the theologian must deal. In the next section, an attempt will be made to exhibit the underlying structure of Christian prayer generally, in the light of which the varieties of prayerful acts engaged in by Christians can be said to derive their meaning and vitality.

THE FORMAL STRUCTURE OF PRAYER

To gain an understanding of the underlying structure of prayer is to acquire a framework both for interpreting prayer in its various forms (praise, thanksgiving, confession, petition, intercession, commitment) and for judging the relative degrees of adequacy or inadequacy about each prayerful act. Bringing into view its formal structure should enhance considerably the comprehension of what is in actuality a highly complex and comprehensive endeavor, in and through which believers learn to seek nothing less than their fullest response to God's presence (or their sense of God's absence) in their own lives. Prayer in its essence expresses the whole of the gospel, and in its actual embodiments the believer's whole understanding of it, whether adequate or not. The Lord's Prayer is an interesting illustration of this relationship between prayer and faith, although it will be argued later that this particular prayer is not without its own structural difficulties.

In the words "hallowed be thy name," believers have received from their Master a vehicle by which to render articulate their developing sense of God's praiseworthiness, their adoring response to that Holy One to whom alone every conscious creature's unqualified homage is due. By the words "Our Father in heaven," with which the prayer begins, it becomes possible to acknowledge thankfully the order of being generally; all things, both visible and invisible, as the Nicene Creed later will affirm, are under the sovereignty of a heavenly being whom man is made bold to address as "Father." Proclamation of God's fatherhood is primarily an act of thanksgiving, of a sort to which Browning alluded in the words of gratitude "God's in his heaven—All's right with the world!" (Tedious theologizing about how the divine attributes truly can be ascribed in finite language, bound in its meanings to the created order alone, has bearing on the concrete actualities of faithful life only if it is informed throughout by the understanding that calling God "heavenly Father" is an act of celebration as well as of classification.) Jesus asked his followers to recognize and express openly, through the words "forgive us our trespasses," their corporate inadequacies whenever they come into the presence of the supremely perfect One. In the church's subsequent history, confession came to assume private forms as well, but always from the prior communal setting. In the almost shockingly specific petition, "Give us our daily bread," believers assure one another of the possibility of individual pleas to the almighty God for the bestowal of both spiritual and worldly benefits, upon request; Jesus did not

45

flinch from encouraging his followers in their natural presumptuousness about the availability of God, even for the mundane task of acquiring daily sustenance. The prayer also provides the vehicle for intercession, the other side of petition, for expressing concern that God will grant benefits not only to oneself, but to others as well: "Deliver us from evil." Through their prayers of intercession (the crucial feature of well-developed prayer life, as will be shown subsequently), believers are to embody love for the neighbor as well as for God; they give explicit witness to participating in a beloved community to whose destiny each is inextricably bound. In daring to make specific requests for himself, a believer soon discovers the naturalness of making them on behalf of others in and apart from the community as well: Deliver *us* all from every bondage which hinders our life together. Finally, by the words "Thy will be done on earth as it is in heaven," that act of commitment to God's own rule is offered which must qualify every address to God; one becomes obedient to God's will as he comes to understand it as an authoritative and benevolent will. Life in obedience proceeds from the trust that all things proceed from grace which is finally incomprehensible, through the power and beneficence of One who has deemed good his every creature and has promised to sustain his creation's goodness from everlasting to everlasting.

Even such a cursory glance at a classic prayer shows that a believer's total response in faith is fully manifest in the language of his prayers. What he understands to be God's self-disclosure will be evident, whether by design or not, in the ways in which he prays or does not pray. In the transition, sometimes anxiety-ridden, from unbelief or prebelief to belief, there is to be experienced a radical alteration in the way one comes to see and affirm things, and the differences between how believers orient themselves in the world become transparent in the language of

rs. It is one's prayers
eself or by someone
s that reality is sup-
s. Do his prayers as
e nature of things,
in isolated moments
oth in tone and con-
ns whose fulfillment
o one's prayers con-
on earth as well as
tend toward limpid
present beneficences,
y which displays no
y future into which
ot? Do these prayers
y about them, or are
they mired in self-pleading mixed with wholly abstract
expressions of gratitude and merely courteous references
to God's holiness? The presence of an intercessory dimension to prayer is the altogether critical dimension; its con-
spicuous absence over the course of time should provoke
the question of whether the other-than-self genuinely
matters to the purported believer, whether he is able
truly to see his inhabited world as a neighborhood.

A believer's prayers make plain how he understands
his environing world, the totality of things, persons, and
relations which impinge meaningfully upon each individual and help to shape the individuality which comes to
be his. Through his prayers, a believer exhibits whether
or not he regards his environing world as worthy of his
deepest concern and heir to an important future. Further
still, they make explicit his own self-understanding in the
faith, whether or not he grasps the fundamental judgment
passed upon him by God, that he is both inadequate to
and called out for creative engagement in God's own
ordering of all things. No one's inadequacies are quite the

47

same as another's, General Confessions to the contrary notwithstanding. Each human being's sinful condition is uniquely his; each in his own peculiar circumstances does what he ought not and does not what he ought. But each is accepted for what *he* is, with his unique deficiencies, and called to unique mission out of his own peculiar situation. Whether a believer really knows this is reflected in the tenor of his prayers: How careful is he to confess his own complicity in the "sins of the whole world" in prayer? And what is the tone of the confession? Is it devoid of conviction that God intends to forgive him? Or is it tendered from the side of hearing and acknowledging that his sin has not counted decisively against him, that he is without excuse for failing to participate in God's reconciling purposes for mankind? Since one must admit to sin in some specific way in order to appreciate the graciousness of his sin's being forgiven, whether or not a believer here and now rightly sees himself as both inadequate and yet accepted and commissioned can be determined to a considerable extent by examining how he approaches the task of confession.

Having referred to the primacy of prayer in expressing faith and faith's object, it is now important to attempt a characterization of the formal structure which every act of prayer variously embodies. The first consideration along this line consists of the reminder that prayer is one response (primarily though not purely verbal) to God's self-disclosure which, as such, will exhibit the same pattern exhibited by every faithful response to divine revelation, whether an act of assent, trust, worship, or service. Secondly, every faithful response to God's revelation has about it the character of duality, a conjoining of contrary dimensions of experience which seem constantly in conflict but which together must be held in a unity, whatever tensions may arise from so doing. How faith is at every level an affirmation of contraries, and in this sense is paradoxi-

48

cal, can be illustrated by references to several traditional Christian beliefs: (a) Faith confesses that man is a sinner, deserving the wrath to come, but also is the primary participant in a redemptive process universal in scope. The startling claim that the essence of man is that of forgiven sinner makes one uneasy; if sin is to be taken seriously at all, how can the fundamental fact about man be that he is already accepted by his creator? (b) Faith holds that its founder Jesus of Nazareth is both human and divine, that nothing less than both affirmations provides the appropriate warrant for the message which Jesus called his disciples to announce to the far corners of the earth. Thus, Jesus' God is both eternal, above the vicissitudes of temporal existence, and incarnate, suffering under Pontius Pilate for man's sake. From the first, theologians have been bewildered by the supposition both that eternality, timelessness, is of the divine essence and also that at some point in human history the Eternal fully entered time and became subject to its conditions. (c) Faith affirms that history is both the locus of human creativity and the stage upon which God is directing his own cosmic drama of redemption. Thus, though man can impede the workings of providence, he cannot destroy its effects altogether. Theologians have never settled the difficult question of how history can be both man's and God's dominion; the paradox persists. Finally, (d) believers regard the church as both a human institution and the Body of Christ; in contemporary terms, the church is properly described from the perspectives both of sociology and dogmatics. But how in the same apparent organization actions could proceed at once from human motives and by divine will defies easy comprehension. These examples represent only a few of the paradoxical kinds of statements believers have felt constrained to make from the outset. Serious questions have been raised about these and all other paradoxes. But none of the considerations

49

brought to bear is likely to provoke believers to reduce the paradoxicality of their beliefs. That faith requires an entering into paradox seems unquestionable.

Every faithful expression of God has about it a paradoxical character in the sense that it maintains in delicate balance convictions and experiences which seem to negate one another even as they demand affirmation. It would seem that, for whatever reason, God has disclosed himself in such a way that all accounts of his revelation must forever be confounding to normal ways of thinking and speaking, paradoxical in the sense that they always have to do with that which runs counter to expectation. (It is not clear, contrary to what many seem to believe, that by paradox must be meant that which is self-contradictory in a logical sense.) In his genuine and gracious self-revelation, God nevertheless remains partly obscure and unapproachable, and wholly incapable of being manipulated; in his most intimate personal encounters with man, God also retains his essential mysteriousness. His fullest self-disclosure in Jesus Christ is for the sake of mercy quite unfathomable ("And can it be that I should gain an interest in the Saviour's blood?"). As Kierkegaard rightly saw, Jesus is both the exalted and the humiliated One; only in relating to this strange phenomenon on these paradoxical terms can one begin to approach the sovereign majesty of God.

The foundational paradox which all Christian prayer must express is the encounter of the believer with a God who retains his transcendent holiness in and through his becoming accessible to human designs. Any and all fully developed prayer will intensify the believer's consciousness of and relation to both the divine holiness and the divine availability. Every believer is taught to believe both that God is too great to have concern for him, a sinful creature ("O thou who art more wonderful than the eyes of man can behold") and that this very same Most Holy One draws near to him to fulfill his requests ("Ask, and it will be given you; seek, and you will find; knock, and it will be opened to you"). The task of prayer, in its desperation and its confidence, is to give expression to this kind of experiential contrariety; to seek to diminish the force of its governing paradox is to deny the very nature of the God who is revealed and to misunderstand the response he asks. Whatever the stylistic merits of any given prayer may be, or whatever may result from it in the world, when it stresses one side of the paradox to the exclusion of the other, prayer fails formally.

Prayer life as a whole and individual prayers fail formally when they articulate content incongruous with their essential structure. An extended engagement in prayer can fail formally if on the one hand it expresses adoration of God and submission to his will to the exclusion of accentuating God's availability to men in concrete circumstances; the One whose thoughts are not man's thoughts and whose ways are not man's ways, who is more remote from man than the heavens are high above the earth, also takes pity upon these his creatures: he is "rich in forgiving." On the other side of the paradox, a practice of prayer can fail formally when it assumes vitality only at critical points in a life which between crises is utterly indifferent to faith (a more serious kind of apostasy than that of antagonism toward faith). When all of a sudden and unexpectedly an individual cries out for a God posited for the occasion, the dignity and honor due the Divine Holiness are annulled; it has not been properly understood *why* God need not at that moment respond to that request on its own terms, no matter how serious or well-intended it may be, and why he is no less caring for choosing not to be claimed by the plea.

Individual prayers can also fail formally. Believers who

seriously petition that it not rain on the Sunday school picnic make a mockery of the Divine Holiness. Contrariwise, those whose prayers are always after the fashion of "Let all be according to thine inscrutable decrees" really blaspheme in refusing to acknowledge God's own stated desire for meaningful dialogue with men, a dialogue frequently permitting even negotiation (cannot contemporary believers wrestle with angels, too?). In all these and related cases, the fundamental criterion by which one can determine the faithfulness of prayer is whether or not prayer exhibits in its own language the paradoxical and mysterious unity between God's holiness and his accessibility.

It is instructive, for illustrative purposes, to apply this criterion to the previously elaborated Lord's Prayer, especially its reproduction in Matthew's Gospel.

> Our Father in heaven,
> thy name be hallowed;
> thy kingdom come,
> thy will be done,
> on earth as in heaven.
> Give us today our daily bread.
> Forgive us the wrong we have done,
> as we have forgiven those who have wronged us.
> And do not bring us to the test,
> but save us from the evil one.
> —Matthew 6:9-13, NEB

Structurally speaking, this version of Jesus' exemplary prayer expresses God's accessibility within a parenthesis which is bracketed on both sides by a correlative accentuating of God's otherness. After stressing the transcendent nature of God's holiness, the prayer begins to look for God at hand: "thy kingdom come, thy will be done, on earth as in heaven." Then the divine accessibility is presupposed without qualification, to provide the day's substance and to protect the faithful from alien powers. The parenthesis closes and the prayer concludes in the same spirit in which it began, with adoration of and submission to God's holy will. In the middle of the prayer, then, are offered confession, petition, and intercession, all expressing personal address to a God who attends to his creatures' every need. At the outer portions of the prayer, presumptuousness gives way to awe in the presence of the all-sovereign and glorious Majesty, from whom and to whom all things in heaven and on earth develop in due course.

Whatever may have been its intent, however, this version of Jesus' prayer upon close examination does not exhibit with requisite clarity the dialectical relationship between the divine holiness and the divine accessibility. For the latter stress occurs only within a bracket in the midst of what is otherwise a hymn of unrelieved praise and adoration to One who is utterly other. Perhaps it was for this reason that it became possible for the liturgy unwittingly to encourage believers merely to repeat unthinkingly the petitions and the intercessions without attempting to translate such statements into terms applicable in their own lives. On the surface, one is led to believe that, if anything, the prayer is too presumptuous; it asks even food from God along with more decidedly "spiritual" benefits (unlike Luke's version which, as was shown previously, enjoins petitioning only for the Holy Spirit). But in this instance what is apparent is not in fact the case; what is most important about the prayer, at the beginning and end, is its awed address to One supposed to be utterly glorious, utterly in control, and utterly beyond all that man needs to communicate. To be sure, part of the prayer is for God's kingdom to come, which seemingly is to concede the possibility that God's will might not be done on earth as it is in heaven; in expressing its *hope* for the kingdom, the prayer seems also to exhibit some confidence that words of address to this effect will indeed make a significant difference to God. But the closing makes plain the overriding conviction that things cannot be otherwise. God's kingdom cannot fail to come; his will cannot fail to be done on earth as it is in heaven; his *is* "the kingdom and the power and the glory, for ever." The serious question which now arises is: How could any creature sensibly seek out a special relationship with One who is already directing all things to a preordained fulfillment? How could it make sense to ask for food when supposedly he already believes that "the earth is the Lord's and the fulness thereof"? How can he think to ask of the Lord that he be spared temptation when he already believes in a God wholly sovereign over all the activities of any reality which man could call "Satan"? If anything prevents this version of the Lord's Prayer from a nondialectical stress upon God's holiness, it is the opening address, "Our Father," which expresses that intimacy which Jesus enjoyed in his own relationship with God, conferred by grace upon all believers. The God whom Jesus dared to address as "Abba" reveals himself also, in Jesus, to be every man's true father. Only this phrase reinstates at all the delicate balance which constitutes the structure of prayer, the polar contrasts by which the divine holiness and the divine accessibility are characterized as a unity, both in reality and in experience.

By contrast, it is instructive to examine the magnificent prayer ascribed to Jesus at John 17, parts of which were quoted previously. It is a prayer of intercession for all those who have and will come to believe in him. More clearly than in the Lord's Prayer is prayer's paradoxical structure here fully manifest. In these words, the early church affirms its conviction that Jesus is one with the Most Holy God, that his intercession before God is that of the "sovereign over all mankind," that his glory is that of the Father before all worlds, and that his destiny is to return to that One from whom he is sent. Having been encountered by him who *is* eternal life, the church also can presume confidence about the future as guaranteed by that very Providence by which all worlds are created and fulfilled; he himself will be with his community of believers, to the end of all worlds. Jesus prays for those with him in this world, that they may become everlastingly one in him. The Most Holy One is also the initiator of a mission whose aim is the enhancement of the whole created order; to such an end nothing less than his total participation shall be given. In Jesus Christ the divine holiness is disclosed in mercy; the Incarnate Word is God's own accessibility in complete union with his perfection.

THE INNER DYNAMICS OF PRAYER

It has been maintained throughout this book that prayer expresses the whole response of faith to what a community believes with its very existence to be revelatory disclosures; prayer is faith's articulation of its total perspective on things. In this section, the task is to explicate the constitutive features of the activity of prayer, noting especially that its richness derives from the magnitude of that reality to which the entire phenomenon of faith seeks a more adequate response.

1. *Adoration and praise* arise in part from awed acknowledgment of the holiness of God, God's otherness from the created order. Prayers of praise are addressed to One who has become an all-commanding object of loyalty and attention by virtue of his unsurpassable worth, worshiped because of his supreme goodness and not because of his threatening and all-consuming power. To emphasize in this way the worthiness of God is not to question the sufficiency of God's power to effect his will for his

creation, a reality beyond doubt for any believer; it is merely to underline that sheer power, even that by which the worlds were made, is not itself the object of adoring worship. As Leibniz rightly saw, in his attempt to deal with the problem of evil:

People have pleaded the irresistible power of God when it was a question rather of presenting his supreme goodness, and they have assumed a despotic power when they should rather have conceived of a power ordered by the most perfect wisdom. . . . Our end is to banish from men the false ideas that represent God to them as an absolute prince employing a despotic power, unfitted to be loved and unworthy of being loved.*

What is praiseworthy about God is the inviolable moral integrity with which he exercises his sovereign power, by which alone he is deserving of the ascription "that than which nothing more perfect is conceivable." The good news about God is that he is the supreme embodiment of all that is conceivably perfect, whose all-sufficient power graciously is creating realms of unsurpassable value. Worship of such a being is worship of One than which none is more deserving of human accolade:

I will extol thee, my God and King,
    and bless thy name for ever and ever.
Every day I will bless thee,
    and praise thy name for ever and ever.
Great is the Lord, and greatly to be praised,
    and his greatness is unsearchable.

One generation shall laud thy works to another,
    and shall declare thy mighty acts.
On the glorious splendor of thy majesty,

* Gottfried Leibniz, *Theodicy*, ed. Diogenes Allen (Indianapolis: Bobbs-Merrill, 1966), Preface; I, 6.

and on thy wondrous works, I will meditate.
Men shall proclaim the might of thy terrible acts,
    and I will declare thy greatness.
They shall pour forth the fame of thy abundant goodness,
    and shall sing aloud of thy righteousness.

The Lord is gracious and merciful,
    slow to anger and abounding in steadfast love.
The Lord is good to all,
    and his compassion is over all that he has made.

All thy works shall give thanks to thee, O Lord,
    and all thy saints shall bless thee!
They shall speak of the glory of thy kingdom,
    and tell of thy power,
to make known to the sons of men thy mighty deeds,
    and the glorious splendor of thy kingdom.
Thy kingdom is an everlasting kingdom,
    and thy dominion endures throughout all generations.

The Lord is faithful in all his words,
    and gracious in all his deeds.
The Lord upholds all who are falling,
    and raises up all who are bowed down.
The eyes of all look to thee,
    and thou givest them their food in due season.
Thou openest thy hand,
    thou satisfiest the desire of every living thing.
The Lord is just in all his ways,
    and kind in all his doings.
The Lord is near to all who call upon him,
    to all who call upon him in truth.
He fulfils the desire of all who fear him,
    he also hears their cry, and saves them.
The Lord preserves all who love him;
    but all the wicked he will destroy.

My mouth will speak the praise of the Lord,
    and let all flesh bless his holy name for ever and ever.
                                                —Psalm 145

Once one understands rightly that the Most Holy One
is not merely an all-powerful being who can accomplish
anything, but is the all-worthy One, he overcomes the
tendency to hope that his petitionary and intercessory
prayers will become quasi-magical devices for manipulat-
ing God's power. Genuine faith is relationship with One
who, in whatever he does, whether answering prayer or
not, will act worthily, in a manner befitting his own perfection; words of address cannot be prayerful which petition unworthy things of a God erroneously believed
willing as well as able to do anything. While it cannot
be denied that, given the sufficiency of his power, God
could assist a nation's rise to supremacy in the interna-
tional community, as he *could* assist a football team to
win its homecoming game, it would be wholly inappropriate to suppose that any human being could influence him
to do either. Petitionary prayers to such ends could not be
responsive to the God disclosed as One who cannot fail
to act worthily.

In *The Idea of the Holy* Rudolf Otto characterized
religious experience as such as awesome, terror-struck
confrontation with a Mystery encountered both as seduc-
tive and threatening; somewhat as moths are attracted to
flame, believers are attracted to God, who is *mysterium
tremendum et fascinans.* If the preceding analysis is
sound, however, the adoration of God is an experience
considerably more profound than Otto's depiction would
lead one to believe. For the divine Mystery into whose
presence the worshiper is lured is to be conceived of also
as the embodiment of the highest human conceptions of
goodness; God's exemplariness and not his power is the
source of his attractiveness. In his advent to men, God

58

fulfills their most carefully considered expectations of what a supremely worthy being would be like. All men have some minimal understanding of "a most perfect state of being" which they develop as they learn to image and conceive ideal states of affairs generally. In communion with a religious tradition, some believe they have come to experience the presence of the very being formerly represented by humanly contrived images and concepts; out of such experience they affirm that at least one ideal conception of a perfect state of affairs is embodied in actuality. It is as if human beings labor to formulate an understanding for themselves of what a most perfect being would be like only to discover themselves addressed by none other than that very Being itself, from "outside" the world, in a form personifying the very characteristics previously conceived to constitute perfection according to mere human standards.

It is not without reason, therefore, that Christian faith appears to so many to be mere wish fulfillment. It deliberately speaks of God in terms which conform to one human definition of supreme value; the ideal of a caring, fatherly nurture of all sentient beings is alleged to represent an actual being, everlastingly over and apart from the order also supposedly created by him but known by his works in that created order. Christian experience unabashedly testifies to the event of being-addressed-by just such a Being, whose being is steadfastly affirmed to be independent of human conception, bestowing its richness upon man for man's own fulfillment. To one outside the circle of Christian belief, it often seems that believers simply wish into existence the kind of reality they prefer would exist. Those inside the circle, however, remain confident that such an interpretation is not adequate to the "facts" of their experience, the confrontation with a mysterious but personal presence not of their own conjuring.

Faith also affirms, to be sure, that the Being who is adored because he does indeed fulfill human expectations also discloses himself in unexpected ways which enhance the understandings of perfection which men themselves can devise. God both confirms and advances human expectations of what a Most Holy Being must be like. By way of example, God has revealed himself both as judge of mankind, by virtue of his moral perfection, and as a redeemer whose desire is to forgive his creatures their striving to become gods in their own right. For reasons of his own, he refrains from holding his creatures fully accountable to the very standards he himself defines as obligatory; he loves his sinful creatures to the end, even as he calls them at every stage on life's way to new and seemingly impossible tasks. Thus, there is something about God's perfection not fully anticipated in man's general understandings of what a most perfect being would be like, were there such; few have ever been disposed to regard absolutions from the obligations of debts to others as an increment to the moral economy.

These considerations to the contrary notwithstanding, however, what elicits prayerful praise of God initially and finally is not startling and unexpected self-disclosures but rather his complete fulfillment of human expectations. God can be praised not because he is more than any human being can imagine but because he is not less. Human beings relate to God in discovering what in God is closest to humanly conceived ideals; their determining relationship with God cannot be sustained with what in God remains remote to human understanding. That which transcends human apprehension can become a relational possibility at all only if it can become embodied in forms comprehensible by man. God's is gracious revelation precisely in the sense that he conforms his transcendent nature to appearances capable of eliciting the possibility of genuine response. Thus, the tradition affirms that precisely in order to make a complete relationship with man possible, God became fully incarnate. The doctrine of the incarnation expresses especially vividly the insight that man can relate fully only to that which accords with those possibilities conceivable within the framework of his own general understanding of things.

2. *Thanksgiving* is an act of explicit recognition, of recalling to present awareness the relationship which God has graciously established with man, in which alone man achieves true humanity. It is the other dimension of a complex act which already includes praise of God's beneficent nature; one thanks God for the specific ways in which his beneficence has been manifest toward human existence. One of the earliest scriptural examples is the cultic credo recorded at Deuteronomy 26:5-9 (NEB):

My father was a homeless Aramaean who went down to Egypt with a small company and lived there until they became a great, powerful, and numerous nation. But the Egyptians ill-treated us, humiliated us and imposed cruel slavery upon us. . . . We cried to the Lord, . . . and he listened to us and saw our humiliation, our hardship and distress; and so the Lord brought us out of Egypt with a strong hand and outstretched arm, with terrifying deeds, and with signs and portents. He brought us to this place and gave us this land, a land flowing with milk and honey.

In these words, gratitude is expressed for the specific benefits which have accrued as a result of God's calling his people Israel; the most profound gratitude, however, is for the covenant itself. While prayers of thanksgiving eventually must direct their words toward some specific act of God's grace, the essence of thankfulness is simply for the creation and man's place in it. Gratitude for the divine-human relationship itself is the theme of the General Thanksgiving which closes the Anglican Morning

Order on a properly eucharistic note: "We bless thee for our creation, preservation, and all the blessings of this life, but above all for thine inestimable love in the redemption of the world by our Lord Jesus Christ, for the means of grace, and for the hope of glory." The prayer's climax sums up the whole meaning of thanksgiving in its request for a continuing sense of the divine mercy in order that "our hearts may be unfeignedly thankful." Thankfulness properly is expressed in a mood neither of awe and reverence nor of fear and trembling. Rather, the mood is childlike, an unembarrassed overflowing of exuberance for the assurance that God has been, is, and everlastingly shall be with his creatures, with grace upon grace abounding in worlds without end. The essential unity (though not identity) of praise and thanksgiving is expressed in the doxological stanza, "We give thanks to thee for thy great glory."

Though "general" thanksgivings frequently are worded in highly formal language for corporate recitation, each individual worshiper's repetition of the same words can and should be highly personal, testifying to the unique relationship established between God and himself which has drawn him into a community at once universal in import and specific in constituency. In the last analysis, prayers of thanksgiving cannot be expressed merely in words of ceremonial homage to a general state of affairs, be it so exalted as that of God's establishment of the cosmos. The General Thanksgiving is misunderstood if it is not seen from beginning to end as a communal chorus of gratitude recited by individuals who know how to mean the identical words uniquely in reference to themselves. In even the most general-sounding prayers of thanksgiving there can come to expression particular encounters with God, a celebration of the astonishing fact that God has chosen to offer unique relationships with each believer in unique communities and that these myriad concrete relationships will be sustained even in his infinitely wider associations in the church and world in all times and places. Thus, even the formalized General Thanksgiving can become a vehicle for articulating one's own particular gratitude that, in Wesley's words, "I, even I, am forgiven and can trust the Lord." Gratitude in this sense does not arise merely from the recognition that Jesus Christ died for all men. From that general statement, of course, one could *infer* immediately that Jesus has died for him. But truly to *affirm* the latter, as Wesley came to understand, requires an act of faith infinitely more profound than that which merely acknowledges the appropriateness of being thankful in general. It is of this more deep-going faith that the psalmist writes:

I give thee thanks, O Lord, with my whole heart;
    before the gods I sing thy praise;
I bow down toward thy holy temple
    and give thanks to thy name for thy steadfast love
        and thy faithfulness;
for thou hast exalted above everything
    thy name and thy word.
On the day I called, thou didst answer me,
    my strength of soul thou didst increase.

All the kings of the earth shall praise thee, O Lord,
    for they have heard the words of thy mouth;
And they shall sing of the ways of the Lord,
    for great is the glory of the Lord.
For though the Lord is high, he regards the lowly;
    but the haughty he knows from afar.

Though I walk in the midst of trouble.
    thou dost preserve my life;
thou dost stretch out thy hand against the wrath
        of my enemies,

and thy right hand delivers me.
The Lord will fulfill his purpose for me;
  thy steadfast love, O Lord, endures for ever.
Do not forsake the work of thy hands.

—Psalm 138

Ordinarily, one first begins to think of the God-man relationship in highly personal terms when he engages in petitionary and intercessory prayer, and not when he thinks about his prayers of thankfulness. That God does hear prayer, that he does respond to petitions directly, usually is entertained seriously only when believers find themselves constrained, sometimes against their most sophisticated understanding, to "take it to the Lord in prayer." But the intimacy of the God-man relationship is disclosed not only at the level of petitionary and intercessory prayer. The highly personal dimension of the God-man relationship must be established for the believer also at the prior level of his prayers of thanksgiving, witnessing that God already has chosen to relate himself individually to each and every one of his creatures and, by doing so, already has established the possibility of each individual's addressing him directly. Prayers of request make sense because, and only because, God has come to each creature already; what otherwise would be a wholly outrageous act of presumptuousness God in his infinite mercy chooses to regard as a consummate act of human faith.

Conceived of in this way, thanksgiving begins to suggest an interesting mutuality about the God-man relationship: specifically, that both God's knowledge of man's needs and his capacity to address them partially depend upon whether or not the relationship has been entered into freely from both sides. Though human needs are universal, and therefore are knowable by God prior to any relationship with any particular human being, *how* each need is experienced by a particular individual, who is at once a nexus of unique possibilities and a unique future, cannot be encompassed wholly in the general knowledge of things which God has "before the foundations of the world were laid." Each person is constituted in part by the thrust of his present decisions, which to some extent at least are free, creative and unpredictable; he is not now what he will be and therefore cannot now be known in his future fullness of being except as one for whom several possibilities are open. Knowledge of what any individual is, as he becomes, will depend partly upon entering an empathic relationship with him, through which the inquirer may come to feel something of the other's decision-making *processes,* but never in a way which would permit easy projection of how those processes will work themselves out. For what that individual becomes is conditioned partly by how he experiences himself as known, empathically, by another. Since neither a decision nor its outcome can be altogether certain, then, those decisions which ground individual self-identity cannot be foreknown wholly, even by God. God knows them, too, only in relating himself to the individual who makes them in such a way that he can come to share something of the unique perspective from which they are considered. In this light, what truly should occasion believers' thankfulness is not the grandeur of One who knows and does all. Rather, the most profound thanksgiving proceeds from the recognition that that same One has chosen to know individuals and their requests concretely and personally by entering into relationships with them; he is not confined to a timeless perspective on the whole which knows individuals only as clusters of features which all individuals share in common. Thankfulness is not for the all as known by God but for one's unique place in what God knows. The wonder is that God never seems to look elsewhere for more interesting and suitable relation partners, unlike these same creatures, for whom not even God in his majesty seems to suffice as a constant guide for their lives.

3. Prayers of *confession* also are acts of recognition. What is recognized, however, is not the relationship with and among men intended by God, but the brokenness of that relationship, brought about by sinful creatures once unwilling and now unable to bear fully its obligations. Confession seeks to bring into the open human deficiencies before God which ought not to be evaded any longer.

Clearly, a confession either of an act or the entire condition of sin does not inform God of anything of which he is not now aware. Neither a lurid and leering exposure by the most depraved nor a muted and hesitant recounting by the most respectable in any sense takes God by surprise; their religious value lies elsewhere. God already knows the alienation of the human spirit and the countless acts of disobedience of which each human being is guilty and to which each is prone better than any sinful creature can ever know. The point of confession, then, must be to enhance one's own self-understanding as a participant in a relationship graciously offered by God without prior conditions. Confession must lay bare all that one ordinarily would seek to obscure, every illusion one harbors about himself, in order to enhance the integrity of the relationship which God seeks to sustain with men in "all sorts and conditions." Only the willingness to bring to full awareness with uncompromising honesty what one really knows about himself and what one desires to harbor secretly can enable man fully to respond to the new relationship offered by God.

However deeply one may be troubled by his shortcomings in the sight of God, though, he can confess his condition, even to himself, only if he is able to believe that his "manifold sins and wickedness" are not the sum and substance of his being, the final assessment of his creaturely worth. Confession is genuinely possible only to one who has considered the announcement of God's grace, who can entertain the possibility that his self-abnegation, however appropriate at the moment, nevertheless does not say all that is to be said about himself. Though he may still mutter inconspicuously the words of a General Confession while he worships with his fellow believers, he cannot mean them genuinely in their specific import for his own life unless he feels *some* assurance that deserved condemnation will not be the last word pronounced upon him. He who truly and earnestly confesses *his* sins already has experienced something of that divine grace in the presence of which he hears the prayer for pardon or the words of assurance. Earnest confession can be articulated only from the stance of believing in the readiness of God to forgive all whose confessions are to be offered. In neither a psychological nor a theological sense can confession ever become the condition for forgiveness; only knowledge of a significant Other's capacity and willingness to forgive makes it possible for anyone to confront his own imperfections candidly. Frequently, liturgies obscure this truth: for example, those which proceed from the General Confession either to the announcement that sins are forgiven or to a prayer for pardon (or, worse still, to an absolution given by the clergyman). But only upon some prior understanding that sins are forgiven can any believer develop the courage and the will to look deeply within himself precisely to that which requires God's gracious act of forgiveness in the first place.

That the transcendent One is a forgiver of sins entails that God is infinitely more than merely an exemplar of values. That God can and does forgive sin must mean especially that his being is not exhausted by its conforming to human expectations of what a supremely perfect being must be like. God is also sovereign *over* all that is conceivably perfect in human terms. Because he is, he possesses authority to dispose all that men revere for their own greatest good, even if the love with which he so acts requires setting aside standards of judgment which otherwise might be determinative in a given situation. He is "beyond" human conceptions of good and evil precisely but only in the sense that he is able and willing to grant dispensation even to those who consciously and consistently refuse to emulate what they know to be the highest good. But it does not follow that God *utterly* transcends what man can conceive as good and evil, that his will and ways are wholly incomprehensible in essence; upon this extreme view, God could only be thought of as capricious and untrustworthy. While it is understandable why such a belief is widely held, usually by sincere believers who are gripped intensely by the idea of God's sovereign majesty, an unqualified stress upon divine transcendence nevertheless compromises for the sake of God's holiness his own self-disclosure as accessible to man.

What confession does point to is a standard of perfection which transcends human powers to formulate precisely, in the application of which God is bringing about an even higher good for man than human understandings of good and evil can envision. Faith's term is "mercy," of One who is seeking to share his own perfection with even the most undeserving, One who became incarnate to suffer humiliation and death's travail for the redemption of that order he himself graciously established for no reason other than love which knew no bounds. To human judgment, it is quite incomprehensible that the order of things generally should include mercy as well as justice; every human rule of law is threatened with disruption at the very center by any suggestion that things may not come eventually to their *deserved* end. But confession points to mercy as integral to God's doings within the created order.

Since God does indeed grant dispensation even to the most merciless of sinful beings, every human conception of good and evil must point to a transcendent embodiment of perfection which to this extent defies human understanding; the term "unsurpassed perfection" must refer to a being prepared to sustain human imperfection even if, according to every conceivable standard of perfection, it is deserving of utter condemnation. The mystery refuses to be penetrated that God could and does actively seek a perfecting of all things according to his own standards of perfection, suspending if need be the application of both humanly contrived definitions of obligation and of his own Torah in order that, according to his own plan of salvation, imperfect creatures yet may be made holy. With Jonah, even the most devout believer often finds it difficult to accept that God does more than judge in accordance with man's highest understanding of order. He cannot quite accept that God intends to nurture him and every other creature to a higher perfection than he feels capable of bearing. But whenever he, too, is provoked to confess his inadequacies, he betrays his own embrace, not by an awesomely transcendent being whose coming is merely threatening (*contra* Isaiah 6) but by One whose loving perfection includes lovingly perfecting the creation, who will bring this about even by setting aside the canons by which it ordinarily is determined what is meet and right to do.

4. Prayers of *petition and intercession* need to be considered as a unity, in that they both have to do with requests for personal intervention by God, whether for oneself or for others. It is at this point that secular Christians can expect to encounter their greatest difficulties with prayer. The request dimension represents the essential difference between believing and not believing; it is an indispensable component in a *living* faith. However, prayers of request contain within themselves all of the most torturous paradoxes accompanying faith generally, intensified to the fullest possible degree. To elaborate

briefly: In the first place, as is the case with respect to prayers of confession, man's requests cannot merely inform God of situations about which he could be presumed ignorant or forgetful; One who notices even a sparrow's fall cannot fail to be aware of every human need. Secondly, believers cannot be in earnest if their aim ever is to influence God to do something he has not already envisioned in his providential design; they know that rhetorical flourish and liturgical correctness do not have this kind of bearing upon the divine benevolence. If man could indeed distract God's attention in the ways some prayerful requests seem to seek ("Dear Lord, help us win this last game for our hard-working, about-to-retire coach"), the object of man's worship would no longer fittingly be named the All-Worthy. Thirdly, however, it must be appropriate in *some* sense to make specific requests to God, even when one is convinced that God is already at work seeking creatively to fulfill man's highest good. Petition and intercession boldly affirm both that one cannot tell God about and influence God to meet any need, and that earnest petitions and intercessions nevertheless will be heard and answered. It is at this point in the life of prayer and faith that the divine holiness and accessibility are exhibited in their most profound unity. Petitionary and intercessory prayers disclose an altogether crucial degree of contingency about the divine-human relationship and the world within which it becomes actual, events within the created order which seem genuinely open to influence by and in that relationship. However strange to secular ears it may seem, a prayer of request tolls the openness of the universe to *miracle*. What can this possibly mean?

Clearly it cannot mean that believers will enjoy material benefits which God denies the unbeliever. Neither the practice of nor the refraining from petitionary and intercessory prayer brings this about directly; prayer seems neither to enhance nor to detract from the worldly gain of either the believer or the unbeliever. It is painfully evident that the rains fall upon men of prayer and secular humanists alike. Further, it cannot be supposed seriously that petition and intercession would bring about interruption of the uniform sequence of events comprising the natural order; otherwise one denies what prayer has already discovered about God, that his love is not capriciously bestowed only upon those who are able to win his favor, no matter how earnest the cause may be for which they plead. While one ought not to be insensitive to a vivid personal testimony that God intervened directly to reverse the terminal direction of an illness (cirrhosis, say), it is perilous in the extreme to build one's whole understanding of God and the world on the basis of such "data." The possibility of a single divinely effected interruption of the natural course of things raises the intolerable question of God's possible direct involvement in every natural occurrence, the horrendous implication of which would be that God has considered and decided against every prayer which goes unanswered. One cannot regard as God's good news an isolated account of a miraculous cure if he knows of thousands whose suffering remains, whose lives also he is compelled to believe governed by God's creativity directly.

What is in fact open in experience to divine influence is the strength and constancy of faith itself; upon being petitioned, either on one's own behalf or for someone else, God has promised to act to enhance believers' powers of persisting faithfully, especially in circumstances burdened by tragedy, even those which seem outrageously unjust, fraught with seemingly senseless pain and anguish. The abundant testimony of the faithful is that the integrity of individual and corporate belief can be and is heightened as a result of prayer. Further still, God's empowering of faithful response is in these instances *dependent upon* prayer. The spiritual consequence of prayer is analogous to what transpires in the process of sanctification, in which believers strive and move toward perfection. Though sustained throughout by divine grace, the effects of this process too are dependent partly upon human responses; though man is forgiven his sins independently of what he does and is, he becomes "holy" only through conscious acts cooperative with God's holy will. Co-creativity of this sort, essential for the fulfillment of God's reconciling work in the created order, is disclosed especially clearly through prayers in a particular time of trial for a sufficiency of faith.

It is largely impossible for secular believers any longer to petition God directly to stop a war or to prevent forevermore earthquakes along the San Andreas fault, though even the most secularized may be driven to do so given sufficient provocation. It is not inconsistent with a generally secular outlook, however, to petition for uninterrupted experience of God in and through every ordeal, in the expectation, aroused by God's own promise, that any such prayer will be heard and acted upon at the throne of grace itself. In covenanting with the community he himself called into being that he will uphold his own through whatever may befall, God has made himself accountable always to be "a very present help in time of need." He himself makes it properly a part of the faithful life to request fulfillment of his own promises in specific situations. There is no reason for any believer to suppose that God intends to answer prayer in ways other than by increasing faith. But the experience of faith testifies to a God who is a resource for human life, whose supportive activities frequently are "on demand," directly dependent upon his receiving man's petitions and intercessions.

If God does not interrupt the normal course of events in order to fulfill a personal request in its own terms, it is not likely that he will do so in order that someone else may benefit from another's intercession. Instead, the effectiveness of intercessory prayer, about which also faith has no doubt, rests with God's power to kindle the imagination and energize the will of the intercessor himself, in order that he may become the agent through whom the other's needs may be addressed. Genuine intercession is the act by which believers become deeply engaged in the very situations occasioning their prayers. Its function is to focus concretely those needs which impinge sufficiently closely upon the believer's own life involvements to enable him to assume part of the responsibility for their alleviation. Because it makes the believer fully aware that the existence to which he is called is under God and toward the neighbor, intercessory prayer is the most important single vehicle by which he can participate in God's own reconciling of estranged mankind. Interceding on behalf of another, in the sense of assuming the burden of bringing about that very thing for which one prays, is the true continuation of the incarnation in human history. God's own power sustains everyone who is so engaged.

5. The language of *commitment* provides the vehicle by which believers are enabled to express that unqualified loyalty to God which is faith at its deepest level. Through whatever good or evil may be his lot, the man of faith is called to an obedience which knows no exception; he will remain only at the periphery of the kingdom unless he learns to commit his life wholly to the righteous will of his creator.

Nevertheless, the tradition has tended to proclaim with excessive zeal that "submission" to God is the highest Christian act because it manifests unmistakably man's utter dependence upon God for all things. The implication is that man has no will of his own, can never be truly a causal agent in his own right. On the contrary, however, to suppose oneself capable at all of affirming "Not my will but thine be done" gives clear expression to the fact that man does have a will capable of functioning independently of God's will, by which he can be either a rebel against or a full participant in God's redemption of creation. It makes no sense to teach that human beings must submit their lives to God unless their resistance to that call were also possible. Tradition's emphasis upon God's sovereignty, then, ought not to be understood as an affirmation that God is the sole causative agent in the world. What must be meant instead is that God is the most trustworthy power operative in things generally and that commitment to his benevolent purposes is the most appropriate way of acknowledging fully that trustworthiness. Believing in, and not merely about, God includes obeying his will both for one's own life and for the wider human community of which one is a part.

Commitment of one's life to God's will is genuine to the extent that it remains steadfast without reference to specific conditions which may or may not obtain in the world. Ambiguity characterizes creaturely existence, whether in its fallen or redeemed condition. The problematic character of life in this world persists, even and especially after one submits his life to the all-sovereign Lord. It is especially the committed believer who can look upon the world as an ambiguous sign of its creator at best; the redeemed know with peculiar clarity how out of joint are all things because they are not yet fully of the kingdom of God. Those who have pledged themselves to the "reign of God" remain keenly aware that they are to endure in a world frequently devoid of any sign of that reign, in which evil seems always about to conquer even the most powerful expressions of the good. Trusting in God with one's whole heart never clouds one's vision in such a way that he is able no longer to see the real evils which persist in the world. He is never tempted to the naïveté of supposing apparent evil somehow not to be evil at all. In an important sense, then, things remain quite as they were for the believer, or perhaps worse still; the perduring quality of his commitment to the new aeon cannot be dependent upon how the world now appears to be tending.

Believers do not commit themselves to God because all things point unmistakably to him as their creator; it is not as clear to secular Christians as it might have been to earlier generations of the faithful that the heavens are declaring the glory of God and the firmament is showing forth his handiwork. Genuine commitment does not arise in spite of the way things seem to be either, as if the degree of one's piety were measured by his willingness flagrantly to deny all that reasonable evidence would suggest is true about the world (for example, in the conviction that faith is at combat with the satanic legions wholly sovereign over this world, which struggles merely to escape the claims of the world). Commitment of life develops finally out of the whole complex of intimate encounters which undergird every act of faith and prayer. That One who has constantly made his presence felt in faith, calling human beings to praise, thanksgiving, confession, petition, and intercession, finally comes to be understood as the most fitting subject of continual and unqualified loyalty. Logically if not necessarily temporally, commitment is the culmination of a whole series of prayerful acts and is dependent upon all that has preceded it; the deepest commitment to God becomes possible only as one begins to understand the full implications of his relationship with that God already confronted in his prior acts of prayer. One becomes obedient not because he is intimidated by the divine majesty but because he is nurtured to see the utter worthwhileness of trusting in God's promises in the light of God's entire self-disclosure as creator, redeemer, and sanctifier of man and man's environing world. Human beings are to submit to God finally because of what God has done for them and not on any other terms. The cogency and persuasiveness of the entire divine-human relationship expressed in prayer make commitment the fitting completion of faith, to be strived for in this life and completed in the next.

With this observation, the investigation of the actualities of prayerful life can be drawn to a close. One aim of the analysis has been to show that theologizing about the practice of prayer, if it attains anything like completeness, will bring into view nothing less than the whole response of faith to God's self-disclosures for man's sake. Thus, the collision between the posture of Christian belief and secular consciousness can be exhibited with particular cogency by examining the secular believer's perplexity in confronting Jesus' command to "pray without ceasing." Further specification of this collision requires a closer look at the belief structure of prayer, the task of the next chapter.

CHAPTER 3

PRAYER AND BELIEF

Having considered the actuality of prayer in terms of its setting, essential structure, and inner dynamic, the study now must turn to an examination of the conditions under which any serious practice of prayer could become possible. The emphasis falls upon the term "serious." As has been pointed out previously, not every prayerful utterance is truly worthy of the name. There are unfounded prayers, specifically those which stress either God's holiness or his accessibility but not both. Further, prayers can be engaged in without good reason; people can and do pray, even frequently, without a consciously affirmed purpose for doing so. One has only to think of prayers with which meetings of Congress are opened. Even committed Christians can practice intense and prolonged prayer without understanding clearly the rationale for their behavior.

However, with respect to any action which can be performed without conscious reflection, if it is to make sense it must submit to interpretation and assessment according to specifiable criteria by which all human behavior can be said to be intelligible and defensible. With regard to the life of prayer, every believer must confront seriously the question of what it is which makes his earnest and continuous prayers acts of faith rather than of desperation, addresses to God rather than exclamations born of intolerable pressures. Though what it is which makes sense of prayer need not be explicitly understood along with every prayerful act, it must be present to experience in some sense for the enterprise of prayer to have integrity. The thesis of this chapter is that prayer is possible finally only for those who can believe in the realities to which genuine prayer witnesses, who can believe as true the normative statements which express the essence of faith, such as those contained in the scriptures and in the church's creeds. The fundamental question to be probed is: Which among these beliefs must an individual have particularly strong convictions about in order seriously to pray? What must he believe confidently about himself, the world of which he is a part, and the nature of Transcendent Reality in order to sustain a *life* of prayer?

The belief structure of prayer is crucial for the possibility of prayer because prayer is an act of individuals as well as of communities. Though the prayers of some worshiping community constitute an indispensable undergirding for each member's private prayer life, their significance remains instrumental rather than intrinsic, a means to the larger end of facilitating the individual believer's coming truly to understand himself, the world, and God through the discipline of frequent prayer. The presupposition of the ensuing analysis is that at its most profound level, in the inner life of the individual believer, prayer is an act which expresses one's deepest convictions about the order of things in the form of an act of speaking. Since there cannot be any beliefs incapable of linguistic embodiment (one cannot *affirm* what he cannot *say*), and since, as will be shown, prayer arises out of some set of underlying beliefs, prayer's expression is through the linguistic forms characteristic of beliefs generally. Wordless prayers, whether felt inwardly or expressed outwardly by gestures and postures, are the exception to rather than the norm for prayer life. They are acts of prayer only if they can be said to express that which can also be articulated in language.

Believers know that by their prayers they intend more than merely a recitation of their beliefs. But certainly prayer is not less than an act of believing. The concepts which prayers employ, without which there is no praying at all, point to an underlying set of beliefs without which in turn prayer would make no sense. Because of the intimate relationship between the language of prayer and the language of belief, prayer itself can become the very medium through which the created order comes to embody the realities to which its concepts refer. In prayer, beliefs about reality *become* true in that prayer energizes believers to *enact* their truth in their lives together. Because this is especially so with respect to intercessory prayer, the act of intercession can be said to be the foundational act of faith, which brings every other expression of faith to its proper fulfillment. It is through their prayers of intercession that believers make incarnate God's intended relationship to the human community. Intercessory prayer not only affirms one's belief about God's relationship to another creature, it is the vehicle for God's grace as it transforms its maker into God's own agent on the other's behalf. Properly understood, such a prayer commits the believer himself to intercede in the ways appropriate to the needs of the other. If it truly is in earnest, intercession is also a promise of relevant action by the intercessor himself. As one commits himself to facilitate in the life of another precisely what he has petitioned God to do, his devotional life truly becomes a life of service, in which God's own will is done as the whole creation is subsumed again under man's lordship. The implication here is threatening, in part: One ought to be wary of interceding on behalf of others unless he is himself willing to do what is necessary to alleviate the situation which provoked his prayer in the first place. Genuine intercession cannot be offered seriously for the sake of "the world" as such.

79

Thus, prayer is indeed infinitely more than merely confessing what one believes. Nevertheless, acts of prayer do presuppose and/or entail beliefs which are conceptualizable, in the light of which every specific prayer can be seen to be appropriate or inappropriate. Its highly interior dimension to the contrary notwithstanding, prayer is not an utterly mysterious mode of human behavior which defies categorization in principle; its language admits of definition, interpretation, and evaluation, by reference both to the underlying beliefs with which a prayer is or is not consistent and to the "fruits" of prayer in the whole life of loving service to God through humanity. Though the latter cannot be discussed merely conceptually, there is nevertheless something to be gained by a theology of prayer with a limited focus upon the underlying belief structure. The partial clarification thereby achieved is superior to silence in approaching the phenomenon of prayer. By way of example, if someone were to say that he believes in a God of love but urges through prayer that that God utterly destroy the petitioner's enemies, it would not be inappropriate even for an outsider to remark that that individual is at best confused and at worst unbelieving, even if his memory is preserved in sacred scripture. As the previous chapter attempted to show, prayer can be assessed formally, by reference to the principle of the paradoxical unity of God's holiness and accessibility. It can also be judged adequate or inadequate in its varying dynamic expressions of praise, thanksgiving, confession, request, and commitment. The subject of the following exposition is the way prayer can be scrutinized in the light of its coherence with the belief structure of faith. The underlying beliefs which must be affirmed as true in order to engage in serious prayer are of two types: (1) beliefs about self and world and (2) beliefs about God, to whom all genuine prayer is addressed. Each set of beliefs will be examined in turn.

SELFHOOD AND WORLDHOOD IN PRAYER

There are at least four crucial convictions which any believer must hold about himself and the world if prayer is to be a serious possibility for him. First, he must believe that *he is known fully, as he is and as he can be.* Though this belief points beyond ordinary experiences to a kind of knower transcending the world, in part it is occasioned by experience very much of this world. Every self-conscious being learns early in his development that both over against and with him are other conscious beings capable of transforming him in their own inner experiences into an object both to be heeded and dispensed with as the occasion may suggest. Self-conscious beings are both aided and hindered in becoming persons by the ways others perceive them, sometimes correctly and at other times distortedly. Throughout, their personhood is very much dependent upon their being perceived in *some* way by *some* others. But in no case is any person wholly and adequately understood by another person. Believers, however, experience themselves as fully known by God, that being to whom their faith is finally directed. From that experience they can construe the phenomenon of being-known-by-others as a sign of Being-Known in a transcendent and altogether more important sense. The imperfect images which finite persons entertain about themselves and others point for faith to an altogether accurate representation of every creature, everlastingly held fast in the understanding of One unencumbered by the limitations of finite knowledge, who knows each by name and in essence. Earnest prayers to God presuppose an infinite qualitative difference between God's and man's knowledge of selves and the worlds which make selfhood possible at all.

Man's worldedness—that is, his essential situation of being encompassed by a totality of meanings imposed by other finite creatures beyond his control—precludes that he or any other finite being could wholly understand and be understood by another. Though worldedness is also the condition for there being any meaning at all to man's existence, that very condition obscures both another's self-presentation and how one's own will be apprehended by others; the experiential structures which largely determine for anyone what will have meaning to him (and how it will have meaning) shape in advance how anything *must* appear in his own consciousness and in turn how he will appear to others. Realities reduce to appearances through the interpretation of experience whose own dynamic is operative largely beyond the conscious control of either the interpreters or the realities interpreted. But over against this burdensome situation, prayer expresses the conviction that the misunderstandings which seem inevitable in human experience do not exhaust the possibilities of one person responding to another. He who prays believes himself and others to be understood wholly by One who cannot fail perfectly to understand. To pray is to believe oneself grasped in an attentiveness without analogy in human cognition, to participate in an ineluctable experience of Being-Understood. The activity of prayer does not depend upon some prior conceptualization of God which already has established its possibility. Believers pray because they already possess, or at least hope for, a profound awareness not based upon mere inference that they already are known fully by One who knows all there is to be known. Faith's perspective on things demands that no account of human self-consciousness be considered complete unless it endeavors also to analyze the transcendental conditions of man's experience of Being-Understood, the ground of those decisive and revelatory events in which men come to know that they are known, not only partially by others but completely by a Transcendent Other.

The second belief one presupposes about himself and his world when he prays is that *he is positively affirmed as he is and as he can be*. Prayers of confession express this conviction especially profoundly. Known in all that he is, actual and possible, by One whose exemplariness is starkly in contrast to his own imperfect achievements and condition, the man of prayer is made also to know that, in the consciousness of that Transcendent Other to whom he prays hesitatingly, he and every other human being have been looked upon, thought about, found wanting, but promised a significant future nonetheless. Sinners remain convinced that, for all of their and others' deficiencies at the very center of their being, they continue to matter to One who alone can reckon their respective value decisively. The One to whom alone anything can matter, make an important difference, has deemed the human race worthy of his redemptive concern to the end time. It should now be wholly apparent that, for the believer, the Transcendent Object of prayer is through and through personal; the grace which makes faith possible is comprehended and comprehensible only as proceeding from One who cannot be other than an eminent Person, a Being who perfectly exemplifies every quality which human beings understand in their imperfectly embodied finite forms to be *personal*. Believers who pray cannot entertain seriously a notion of divine reality, for example, as mana, universal energy, for no such concept can do justice to their incorrigible conviction that they are known-and-assessed, that their very being is upheld by a relation of being-known-and-loved-by that very One whose judgment alone could truly matter to anything's well-being. Mana is not the kind of reality for which "making judgments" or "being-significant-to" has any meaning; mana can neither discover nor make anything significant. (And so much the worse for mana.)

Third, the man of prayer must believe that *his Being-*

Known and Being-Loved is a relationship constantly re-affirmed in the present experience of the Transcendent Knower. While earnest prayers arise primarily from a community's remembrance of divine beneficence in its own past, their most important function is as vehicles for its relating to God in the present. Believers cannot rest content to employ prayer for the sake of celebrating merely the steadfastness of God's unalterable design, as if before the foundations of the world were laid God had already anticipated and made an irrevocable assessment of all that would transpire in due course, making unnecessary any modifications in his relationship with his creatures as a result of their own creative participation in the historical process. Instead, faith-filled prayers boldly affirm that God's knowing and assessing take place in the present as well, and that divine cognition construes the present order in the light of a future yet to unfold. God's responsiveness to prayer especially manifests the depth of his commitment to create possibilities for mutually enhancing relationships between himself and the created order. The intensity of the dialogue generated by prayer points to the most important single feature of the God-man relationship, its orientation to the future. For man and for God, there is much yet to be known and appreciated about created beings, for there are untold possibilities yet to be actualized in some way both for God and every individual to whom God comes. How they will come to fulfillment remains to some degree indeterminate even for the Transcendent Knower of every actuality as actual and every possibility as possible.

Prayer, then, presupposes considerably more than a sharing in the effects of past acts of grace; it is a here-and-now response to the experience of presently Being-Known and Being-Affirmed. In prayer one becomes explicit about his expecting to reap the harvest of faith anticipated in the community of faith from the outset. And he expects of that harvest that it shall be both genuinely fresh in itself and nourishing for the future which God and his beloved community will create together, a future whose outcome neither men of prayer nor the Transcendent Being can fully anticipate. Insofar as he prays at all, the man of faith does not believe merely that once long ago he was known and affirmed positively. He also believes that his present state of being is also a datum for God's understanding at this moment in time. Prayer cannot be serious if it is addressed to One whose understanding is atemporal, which abstracts from the concreteness of contingent things universal characteristics cognized only in an eternal vision of an unreal whole. In an eternal present, one who could intuit things according to their universal dimensions only could not embrace lovingly the essentially temporal order to which finite things truly are bound. Prayer, however, supposes instead that God becomes increasingly active with every passing moment in establishing and sustaining relationships with each thing as it comes to be, exhibiting throughout an infinite power of attentiveness beyond every finite creature's capacity fully to comprehend, through which every one of God's creatures, past, present, and yet to come, enriches his concrete life to the end of all worlds.

Finally, prayer expresses the conviction that *the world constitutes the horizon within which every creature is known and assessed.* It is a false expectation of prayer, unsupported by experience of true faith, which demands of it ecstatic moments transporting suppliants wholly beyond the domain of ordinary consciousness and life. Prayer betrays rather that divine revelation always occurs within a matrix of worldly involvements; God discloses himself to worlded creatures precisely in order to illumine their very worldliness in judgment and mercy. He comes to men as their creator whose advent seeks to restore and not to annul his creation. He never points to a pathway leading away from the world; that very world he has always deemed good. His Word became flesh and dwelt among us. God's self-disclosures are always in and for the problematic of some particular situation; thus, an appropriate response in faith seeks self-consciously their import for worldly endeavor, aiming always toward enhancing man's participation in the world rather than in a kingdom wholly other than the world. Faith cannot genuinely be a response to revelation if it is accompanied by diminished interest in the relationships which obtain in the world.

It cannot be denied that there are times during which withdrawal from worldly disarray is necessary for the very practice, much less the development, of prayer life; prayer frequently requires solitude. Nonetheless, as Jesus' own example shows clearly, solitude is rightly for the sake of renewing one's strength for worldly responsibilities; unless it aims toward a more creative participation in the world from which one temporarily detached himself, prayer reduces to an escape mechanism whose inner essence flagrantly denies the grace of God itself. It is God's design that man "be" at all only in an environing world; he who does not pray consciously from the perspective of some world, for that world, has not yet comprehended who it is who calls him to faith and thus has not yet responded truly to that call in faith. God reveals himself to human beings for the sake of enhancing their possibilities for wider and deeper involvement in their own worlds.

Prayer requires of any interpretation of the human environing world that it be conceived to include the meaningfulness of man's relationship with Transcendent Reality. If the cosmos is to be understood at all, faith demands, it must be understood as somehow supportive of the possibility of such a relationship; the man of prayer believes that the framework by which all occurrences within the cosmos are interpreted should be formulated

86

accordingly. For him, the cosmos is incomprehensible in its essence unless some attempt is made to characterize the structures which make such transcendent relationships possible. By way of contrast, Bertrand Russell once offered one of the most sobering and moving accounts in contemporary literature of secular man's tendency to view the universe as either hostile or neutral to the human venture:

That Man is the product of causes which had no prevision of the end they were achieving; that his origin, his growth, his hopes and fears, his loves and his beliefs, are but the outcome of accidental collocations of atoms; that no fire, no heroism, no intensity of thought and feeling, can preserve an individual life beyond the grave; that all the labours of the ages, all the devotion, all the inspiration, all the noonday brightness of human genius, are destined to extinction in the vast death of the solar system, and that the whole temple of man's achievement must inevitably be buried beneath the debris of a universe in ruins—all these things, if not quite beyond dispute, are yet so nearly certain, that no philosophy which rejects them can hope to stand. Only within the scaffolding of these truths, only on the firm foundation of unyielding despair, can the soul's habitation henceforth be safely built.*

Over against every such picture of hopelessness, however, men of faith and prayer claim to see a perpetual unfurling of transcendent possibilities for the human future. How this can be becomes the fundamental question for any and every cosmology; that the cosmos is malleable to human designing under the inspiration of a transcendent creator is still *the* fundamental insight which any cosmology must explicate if it is to be true to its subject.

* Bertrand Russell, "A Free Man's Worship," *The Basic Writings of Bertrand Russell,* ed. Robert E. Egner and Lester E. Dennon (New York: Simon & Schuster, 1961), p. 67. Copyright © 1961 by George Allen & Unwin, Ltd. Used by permission.

THE GOD WHO HEARS PRAYER

The first set of convictions which make the practice of prayer a serious possibility had to do with believers' own self-understanding. The second set exhibits conceptually the characteristics of that Transcendent Reality which enable a hearing of and a responding to believers' addresses. The first set answered the question: What must be true about the believer and his world if his practice of prayer is to be worthy of serious consideration? The question to which the second set of beliefs comprises an answer is: What must be true about God if prayer is to be an effective medium of communication with him? First, that Transcendent Reality referred to by the word God is *responsive to what is personal in man and in this sense is personal in himself.* Christian prayer can make no sense unless one supposes that the One to whom it is addressed is not "it" but "he" (or even "she," although it is not a concern of this study to argue for or against theological expressions of the cultural phenomenon disparagingly deemed "male chauvinism"; the altogether more important point is that whatever is responsive to personal existence cannot be other than personal, however more than personal one may wish to say that Transcendent Reality is).

Concerned to discover suitable substitutes for the admittedly cruder forms of anthropomorphic expression which seem to pervade the original testimonies of faith—for example, Jacob's nocturnal wrestling bout with Yahweh—theologians have tended to gravitate toward highly curious ways of speaking about God which are not readily grounded in the experience of faith itself. For example, God frequently is spoken of in seemingly contradictory terms as *infinitely* more than personal, yet not impersonal or nonpersonal. Tillich once spoke of a "God above God" who is Being itself and not *a* being. Contrary to the intentions of those who employ them, however, such expressions entail that what is said to be personal in God really is an appearance only of an incomprehensible whole which is transpersonal in infinite measure, which finally is to say that God is not a person at all, not to be addressed as "Father." To think of God not as *a* personal being but as the wholly mysterious Ground and Source of Being, beyond description according to the categories pertinent to understanding the finite order, is to deny faith's affirmation of the ultimacy of personal reality.

Several indispensable corollaries accompany belief in *a* personal God. As personal, God must be conceived as a conscious being as well, with every conscious being possessing the capacity to distinguish between what is uniquely himself from what is other than himself. As a person, all God's relationships are *conscious* relationships which exhibit both the reality and the understanding of the self/not-self polarity at the heart of things. In that conscious states depend for their very being partly upon what is other than themselves—they "are" at all only as distinguished from those others—it would appear that God too must be conceived as at least partly dependent in his being upon his conscious relationships with created things. Whatever the traditional doctrine of God may say to the contrary, prayer very much presupposes the power of creaturely beings to affect God qualitatively; in that prayers matter to God at all, his own concrete actuality must in part be conditioned by the quality of relationships sustained with his creatures. God experiences the created order in a new way when prayers are addressed to him; in this sense, that which was the case with respect to God's own inner life is no longer the case whenever someone prays. No speculative ontology of Being and Non-Being is required to support this view: it is from the experience of

God as personally responsive to believers' needs that his consciousness and conscious dependency on all that is other than himself can be inferred.

Prayer supposes, then, that God is a being who perceives, conceives, and judges. Clearly it is the first part of this claim which poses the greatest difficulty: the unnerving suggestion that God both receives and responds to stimuli from the physical order. The only way in which it could make sense to say this is to ascribe corporeality to God; it is not coherently conceivable that any being could "hear" auditory stimuli through which verbal meaning-complexes are transmitted unless that being is equipped with sensory receptors of some material sort (even if it is an *extra*sensory receptor). Unless it is sheer equivocation to speak of God "hearing" and "answering" prayer, it is difficult to avoid the conclusion that God, too, is in some sense an embodied being. It may be of some comfort, albeit very little, to remind oneself that divine corporeality may be *quite* different from any corporeal form now humanly conceivable. What cannot be supposed, however, is that God's corporeality is *utterly* unlike man's.

The difficulties in thinking about God as a personal being lessen once the stumbling block of affirming God as a perceiver is overcome. Traditional theological thinking has not hesitated to ascribe the power of conceptualization and judgment to God. Both for man and God, these have to do with interpreting representations of the world through comparison and contrast with other abstractions from experience retained in memory. Presumably, God's conceptual powers in this regard differ from man's infinitely, but in infinite degree rather than kind; unlike man's, God's field of comparison is unlimited, spanning the whole of reality, actual and possible. It cannot be overstressed, however, that in no case is it possible to conceive and formulate judgments about *anything real* without prior perceptual experience; God cannot know his creation at all if his knowledge is wholly independent of experiencing concretely the contingent particulars in that order. A timeless vision of a system whose interrelationships are all necessitated from the outset cannot be of that order which human beings experience, even though classical doctrines of God have portrayed God's knowledge of the world in precisely this abstract way.

Finally, if God is a personal being, it must be *literally* true to say that he understands and uses language. Scripture and tradition are replete with "symbolic" statements about the divine Word; but language about that Word must be more than merely figurative expressions of a reality wholly other than what the term "word" ordinarily suggests: namely, meaning complexes communicable between finite conscious beings. It would be absurd, of course, to suppose that God requires in order to communicate with himself and with his creatures any particular language exclusively, as if God might not understand the work of Augustine, for example, because he uses Sanskrit but not Latin. Since, however, there are no wordless prayers in principle, in that what constitutes an act as prayerful is its translatability into some verbal expression congruent with the belief structure of faith, prayer cannot make sense unless in some way God *does* employ human languages. What seems to be suggested is that the linguistic medium within which God communicates is one into which every earthly vernacular can be rendered. Language is *the* distinctive medium for personal self-expression and communal life in human experience; hence, God cannot be a personal being and not be a competent user of language (an omnicompetent linguist, it is tempting to suppose). Only through language does God show forth his all-sovereign purpose that all shall be saved, that his will shall be made known in every region on earth.

His kingdom will come as human beings testify to it in their many tongues, each earthly vernacular capable of mediating the divine presence. As is well known to the Christian community, from the day of Pentecost each shall hear the voice of the Lord in his own language. In sum, the transcendent One to whom men pray must be believed to be, as he is experienced to be, a responsive Presence to all that is distinctively personal in human existence.

The second belief about God which must be presupposed by one who prays earnestly is that *God is genuinely affected by the world to which he discloses himself*. To expect any significant outcome to prayer, one must believe that God has entered into covenant to answer prayer, that God has allowed the world to make a difference to him in the sense that what will transpire in the created order shall modify in some measure the character of God's own concrete life. Prayer affirms that God has chosen *not* to remain as he might have been had there been no human environing world at all. Contrary to what the classical doctrine of God stresses in "orthodox" circles, no one can pray seriously who believes that the One to whom he prays remains essentially impervious to any and all transactions with the created order. A God capable of remaining God without creatures to care about is not the all-worthy One in whom believers trust with their whole hearts. While one may be taught to *believe* that there is a wholly transcendent and incomprehensible source of all things who remains eternally unchanged through every exercise of his creativity, one does not lovingly entrust his whole being to such mystery. A God who hears prayer cannot remain identical with his state of being prior to the hearing and the answering of even a single prayer. Rather, the content and tonality of his inner life are genuinely altered in and through the relationships he sustains with faithful men of prayer; both what and how he is depend partly upon how his creatures do and do not articulate prayerfully their responses to his creativity and graciousness.

Most importantly, how he will exercise his sovereignty beneficently in the created order also depends upon the relationships sustained by prayerful dialogue. Only in hearing his prayers can God come to know more fully each believer's own being, for that being is quite literally *not yet* until one gives it expression in a linguistic act such as prayer. Since creaturely being is contingent being, whose every state might have been otherwise, how each man is confronting concrete circumstance cannot be wholly known sub specie aeternitatis, without entering into an empathic relationship within which that man can give his own unique expression to the ongoing struggles of life in all their contingent character. For example, not even God can know fully how one of his creatures is coping with the unexpected and tragic death of a loved one until the sufferer verbalizes his state of mind in various ways, including prayer. How he prays in that situation discloses how he now *is* and therefore conditions how God shall respond to his needs. It makes no sense to suppose that the *concrete* character of God's response was determined prior to the situation which called for it. Prayer illustrates especially vividly that there is something important about even God's being which is contingent, dependent upon circumstances which arise unpredictably in the world of his own making, but to which he is everlastingly related. In and through prayer there develops a continuing enhancement of both man and God; each comes to experience more deeply the actuality and the possibilities of the other. It would seem to follow that there is something perfectable even in God, in the sense that the plenitude of his being increases as responses to him increase throughout the created order through all ages. What that divine fullness of being shall be can be anticipated only dimly, perhaps even by God; it is yet to emerge in and through infinite transactions with his creatures not now even begun.

PRAYER AND CLASSICAL THEISM

The God to whom one prays is an abiding presence who remains open to change in all his relationships with his creatures. By contrast, the God concept in classical theism is formulated with the aid of the philosophical idea of Unconditioned Being, eternal and absolutely self-sufficient, for which any mutual relationship with the created order is in the last analysis unintelligible. As Pascal rightly noted, this "God of the philosophers" is not the God of Abraham, Isaac, and Jacob whom Jesus Christ called Father. Prayer looks to One who draws near to and abides with man, promising to be present continually. God's being is not that of the Absolute but of a gracious presence which throughout sustains care for his creatures. While it may be the case, according to earnest theological reflection upon the experiences of faith, that a God of love cannot fail to be present with man and is in this sense *bound to* rather than *free for* relationships with his creatures, from the standpoint of faith itself, the experience is of gratitude for grace bestowed upon undeserving creatures, without surcease.

Whatever the metaphysical implications may be of trusting in a God whose very being overflows in loving-kindness, when the theologian comes to pray in earnest, he basks with every fellow believer in the wonder of God's presence and boldly speaks in a language remote from that with which he constructs his systems of doctrine. He may assent with his mind to a creedal definition of God as omnipotent, omniscient, eternal, immutable, and self-grounded, but to the extent that his reflective activity continues to be a response to God's own impingement in his

94

faithful life, he should also know how far removed is this kind of utterance from the language by which he addresses God in his own prayers. Much more should be said than usually is admitted in sophisticated circles of the fact that theologians, too, do not usually pray to the "Ground of Being" but to their "heavenly Father."

For good reason, then, many have thought it peculiar that theologians should expend so much effort to demonstrate the existence of God when their own prayers leave no doubt as to their deepest convictions about the matter. In prayer, the God who appears is not the abstract being referred to even in Exodus 3:14: "I am who I am." He is instead "Emmanuel," the One who has come and has promised to remain forever. The abstract concept of a "necessary being," one who cannot fail to be, cannot express adequately the intimate, grace-filled quality of the God-man relationship. The speculative focus is on a being whose essence is altogether independent of man's; the whole point of considering God's "existence" as an intellectual problem is to show God's independence from human desires, needs, and longings, that God is not *merely* an idea in men's imagination. But the Christian understanding of God need not be developed around an exposition of the creeds or the *philosophia perennis*; instead, it must seek to elucidate the kind of Being presupposed by believers in their most serious endeavors to respond faithfully to a Word experienced as a word of address.

In this regard, it should be instructive to attend to two major emphases of the classic Christian doctrine of God in order to see whether they too are or are not undergirded by the actualities of the life of prayer. For it is as important to explicate what prayer does *not* necessarily imply about God as it is to elaborate in detail its positive suggestions. Brief consideration now will be given respectively to the doctrines of creation and the trinity in relation to the understanding of prayer.

Odd though it may seem, prayer does not appear to require that God be thought of as a Transcendent Being who is sovereign over *all* things, "visible and invisible." Though faith does indeed celebrate God's sovereignty and efficacy in the created order, prayer does not necessarily presuppose that God's lordship over all things is *absolute*, in the sense that all that is not God is created by him out of nonbeing (*creatio ex nihilo*). Prayer requires only that he who hears and answers human words of address is capable of strengthening and increasing man's faith; whatever further capabilities he may possess are not disclosed in the situation of prayer itself. Indeed, once the man of prayer begins to conjecture about the availability of wider powers than these, his false expectations about what prayer might accomplish can lead him to the brink of unfaith; he may come to depend upon "signs and wonders" rather than upon God's grace.

That God is able to sustain man's faith in answer to earnest prayer surely constitutes significant data for further inferences about the extent of divine power, and the theological tradition rarely has been hesitant to work these implications out. The condition under which there could be effective granting of prayerful petitions might well be nothing less than God's ordering of the entire cosmos. But it is difficult to see how "creation faith" in its entirety could be inferred from the experiences of prayer. Nothing in the experience of the community of faith suggests that a believer capable of supporting his troubled neighbor is himself insulated from similar crises; no one is capable of controlling the circumstances of his own life so fully that reciprocal support might never be required. The suggestion would seem to be, therefore, that the One who sustains faith in response to prayer well may have unrequited needs unique to his own being. It might be the case that the *permanence* of God experienced in prayer, God's abiding presence, permits some inference to an all-sovereign creator in the classical sense; it could be argued that God cannot remain present to every believer unless nothing were capable of hindering him in *any* way, and that such freedom from external constraint points to his being in control over all things. But the inferential rather than experiential character of this kind of "knowledge" is painfully evident. And on merely logical grounds, the supposition of God's permanent presence does not itself warrant the conclusion that he is *maker* of all things to which he is present.

Such considerations as these need noting because the language of prayer often is weighted heavily with imagery appropriate to the creeds but not to the experiences of faith which give rise to prayer at the outset. The imagery often occasions a facile presumption that prayer should be addressed to a reality conceived altogether differently than "ordinary" prayer language would indicate. But prayers to the all-sufficient, abstractly conceived deity of classical theism reduce the dialogical character of genuine prayer to monologue pitiably directed *at* God without serious hope that intelligible response will and could be heard from God's side.

A second illustration of the point under consideration has to do with the doctrine of the trinity. However frequently believers are encouraged by the church to offer their prayers "in the name of the Father and the Son and the Holy Spirit," the reality designated by these terms does not seem to be present in prayer itself. The concept of God as the unity of Father, Son, and Holy Spirit is at once more abstract and precise than is any concept of the being to whom heartfelt prayer is addressed; the presence of the Transcendent Other in prayer is of a being whose inner complexity (if truly he possess such) is not experienced with anything like the clarity achieved through the several centuries of ecumenical discussion which yielded the creedal definition of the triune God.

Prayer seems to be more of an address to a *single* rather than *unitary* object. Thus, at best, God might be said to appear in one of several ways, in response to different kinds of prayer, disclosing himself at times as creator and sustainer, at other times as redeemer, and on still other occasions as sanctifier. From three distinct disclosures of this sort inferences might be drawn, such as Schleiermacher's, for example, to the tri-unity of God. But the discrete experiences which give rise to such inferential thinking are not easily described, when construed separately, according to the terminology of the classical dogmatic pronouncements of the church ("by the Holy Spirit, through the Son, to the Father"). The point here is not that theologizing regulated by "Hellenistic" forms distorts the authentic experiences of faith. If anything, just the reverse is the case; creedal language has a precision about it for which believers ought devoutly to wish in their own utterances. However purified faith may be by theological reformulations of it, though, the inchoate character of prayer language remains to confound attempts to build precision into it on its own level of expression.

Having characterized briefly the beliefs to which men of prayer are and are not committed, this chapter will seek now to define in broad terms the difficulties which accompany any serious attempt to affirm the belief structure of prayer as a whole. In the next section this task will be taken up in a preliminary way, preparatory to a more considered treatment of the difficulties in the chapter to follow.

SECULAR MAN AND PRAYER

From the outset, Protestantism unwittingly has created among its adherents a sense of deficiency and incompetence about prayer. The cause of the matter seems to be Protestantism's deep-seated and partly justified suspicion of any activity which gives even an appearance of ritualizing the religious life. Rightly or wrongly, the Protestant is taught to believe that no act is a worthy religious act unless it is motivated throughout by conscious religious zeal. By contrast, all that seems formal and external to religious motives is to be dismissed as "Romish" in character, a works-righteousness incompatible with Protestantism's uncompromising stress upon justification by faith alone. Though there are many good reasons for believing that inner integrity is the heart of faithful life, one unfortunate consequence has been that within Protestant communities it has been very difficult to develop a disciplined spiritual life, whereas the Roman Catholic tradition consistently seeks to make appealing and helpful both corporate and individual liturgy by which to structure the life of faith. Catholicism's positive regard for ceremony and formality is virtually anathema within Protestantism.

This has meant that Protestantism has not found a widely appealing way to confront believers' deep-seated need for order in the religious life; only rarely has there ever been any serious attempt to define a pattern of living which would illumine especially the mundane moments of existence between the times of intense religiosity. Protestantism's great strength is its insight into the perplexities surrounding the ecstatic moments of religious experience; its weakness is its inability to guide believers between such moments. Except in its most sectarian communities, the Protestant penchant for authenticity makes virtually impossible any lasting preoccupation with spiritual self-discipline. Concern along this line tends to be seen as an attempt to impose, in Tillich's terms, an alien heteronomy upon a life-style which is ideally theonomous (but is in fact merely autonomous). Thus, one reason why Protestants must feel a sense of lack in their devotional life is their participation in the very ethos which precludes prayerful preoccupation with all of life. In spite of this perennial problem of Protestant piety, however, prayer always has been recognized at least as a possibility, however difficult it may be to sustain actually. A unity of the Protestant principle of criticism and the Roman Catholic principle of substance is still a vision many are capable of sustaining, and with it the hope that every believing community will find ways to encourage the faithful in meaningful and continuous prayer life, even as those same communities continue to engage in the kind of agonizing self-criticism which renders prayer and any pretension to spiritual existence extraordinarily difficult.

The intensity of the contemporary problem with prayer, however, cannot be accounted for merely by reference to certain structural deficiencies within the Protestant heritage. Nor will it do to dismiss the uniqueness of the situation with the all too easy reminder that willful neglect often is the root of spiritual malpractice in every age, secular or presecular. For contemporary Christians often find themselves unable to pray because they no longer can maintain the requisite certitude about the very beliefs which prayer presupposes and implies. As has been maintained throughout these pages, if prayer is an expression of faith, its absence must betoken diminishment of faith at some level. Or to express the correlation in the reverse way, if an individual lacks firm conviction about the beliefs to which faith is supposed to give utterance, he will be unable seriously to invest himself in a continuing life of prayer. It is conceivable, of course, that one and the same person could continue mechanically to pray while admitting to a radical disbelief of everything for which his faith traditionally has stood. Or he may both believe and pray through sheer habit. But though such a person might take himself seriously, no one else should or could do so; one ought not to be regarded as a man of prayer unless he is willing, however falteringly, to confess those beliefs which alone make prayer genuine, independently of the conditioning of his psychosocial environment.

This contemporary crisis of unbelief cannot be understood any longer as one over against which the church continues to stand self-assured. For the crisis is being experienced at the deepest levels of church life as well. Human reality cannot be conceived any longer, if indeed it ever could, as constituted by two communities, the church opposed to all the unbelievers, the faithful within and the pagans or secularists outside. The "established" churches are losing their vitality because many within their own walls now are unable to bring themselves, at those infrequent but decisive moments of uncompromising honesty, to affirm what their churches traditionally have taught. While there are other explanations for the decline of membership within some of these organizations which may be temporarily consoling—for example, the widening gap between clergy and laity on social questions —fundamental to the decline is simply a readily discernible, rapid, and perhaps irreversible erosion of confidence that the beliefs promulgated by the churches really are true.

It cannot be denied, of course, that something of a religious revival continues to arouse the sensibility of multitudes not only in this country but in Western civilization generally; there remains a not insignificant remnant within Christendom still capable of believing that for which Christians through the centuries willingly have died. But that remnant lives increasingly in sectarian societies, deliberately withdrawing from the mainstream of secular civilization generally. Churches of these persuasions are indeed growing while the established churches suffer steady decline, partly because their members vividly set themselves in opposition to much about contemporary life which admittedly is threatening, confrontation with which many would wish to avoid. Who, no matter how secular-minded, has not felt the temptation to denounce secular, scientific, technological civilization as the latest beguilements of Satan? But in spite of their popularity, which it must be conceded evidences no sign of ebbing in the immediate future, all such revivals really shout the last hurrahs for traditional Christianity; their voices are from the cemetery, and they echo the death throes of traditional Christianity. Serious-minded people, alive to and affirmative of the rich possibilities of a scientific, technological culture, are unable for very long to breathe in the sulfurous atmosphere of fundamentalism and pentecostalism.

For better or worse, the responsible Christian is also a secular being; he cannot *not* be a secular being. Often disposed though he may be to revert to a former mode of existence and dismiss secularity as demonically inspired, in the last analysis he cannot help participating vitally in that secular order. But he also cannot be fully himself apart from the religious establishment, and therefore he shares even more deeply than the purely secular person in the crisis of unbelief which is the pervasive feature of contemporary consciousness. The secular*ist*, as opposed to one whose orientation is self-critically secu*lar*, has already achieved an illusory wholeness of perspective by cultivating studied indifference to the claims of organized religion (and unorganized religion as well, for that matter), and he has convinced himself that he suffers no diminishment of human possibilities for so doing. But one who is both secular in outlook and a contributing member of some religious society suffers the untold agony of living between the claims of two sets of meaning complexes (two "worlds") unrelieved by more inclusive insights into how those various meanings might converge; that the secular Christian is one who refuses to disavow either world makes his plight almost tragic.

There are, after all, two kinds of disbelieving. The more

radical expresses unqualified denial of the realities witnessed to by faith. The secular but church-oriented Christian, however, disbelieves in another way; he has come to question the adequacy of traditional faith's representation of those realities, but he does not know how to go about reformulating the representations in a manner commensurate with how he understands things from his contemporary perspective. The church's crisis of disbelief is of this second sort; it reflects growing doubts about the adequacy of its symbols to the divine reality once mediated through them. The church has always known that there are sharp distinctions to be drawn between the object of faith, God, and the conceptual expressions of that object in scripture and tradition, by the preacher, or in ecclesiastical pronouncements ad hoc. But most recently it has come to be felt widely, especially within the church, that though Christianity's traditional expressions purport to be about God, for secular believers they have come to point to different, more remote realities altogether. Hence the secular Christian's disbelief is not a denial of any transcendent object for faith statements at all, of the very realities which faith language seeks to represent, but rather a deep-seated puzzlement about the adequacy of the received tradition's expressions of God. When he questions a theologian's doctrine of God, or rejects a preacher's sermon, or disregards tradition and the scriptures altogether, he need not be construed as dismissing the realities to which such witnesses point.

Distinguishing the realities to which faith responds from the imperfect but genuinely inspired expressions of those realities is mandatory once one becomes aware that faith is man's response to the Divine and is not itself divine. What the Divine is, however, never can be understood except in the terms of *some* response, except as refracted through human experience and articulated in human language and concepts. God is not known in him-

103

self; faith's language always has been a stammering attempt to say something rather than nothing about what in itself partly transcends every finite creature's experience. Both sides of this statement must be carefully noted. Faith is indeed a response to divine reality; it is not merely the work of creative imagination. But that reality is understood only through the interpretative framework in which the response is formulated, whose concepts derive from reflection upon the human environing world. Because every statement about divine reality is made on the basis of experiencing God in and not apart from the world, no faith claims can be said without doubt to express truly what is really divine. Nevertheless, the fact that faith is conditioned through and through by the believer's cultural orientation does not by itself establish that faith builds upon humanly contrived stories "known" not to have any real basis in fact, like those made up on the spot in response to a child's winsome request.

Difficult as the distinction may be to sustain between the reality which occasions faith and faith's conceptualization of that reality, it is the kind of distinction commonly supposed throughout many arenas of inquiry. The distinction crucial to the present argument is that between a sign and the thing signified. When words which could serve many functions successfully point out things to people, they are deemed signs. "Rock" assumes a sign function when users of language employ it rather than some other word to stand for the reality which any particular word *could* name. Whenever people choose not to renew a word's "permit" to point to things, new words come to signify the same realities. This is especially evident with respect to valuing words, more so than with thing words. For example, in recent times the term "integration" has given over to the term "black liberation" by staunch advocates of social reform. Many who are actively working on behalf of racial justice now believe that the vision of a universal human community is expressed more adequately by the latter term than by the former. "Black liberation" advocates argue cogently that the term "integration" really suggests the assimilation rather than the acceptance of black people, contrary to the integrationist's own ideal of a society in which differences would be respected and equality of opportunity ensured.

Faith, too, frequently discovers a need for new language in order to express the divine impingement upon changed circumstances. And sometimes concepts must be reformulated because the reality itself comes to be seen in new ways. A dynamic faith does not tremble at the prospect that even the newest and most daring concepts presently under consideration will be subject to reassessment in the future for reasons which no one can fully anticipate at the moment; faith knows that to replace one image or concept by another is not necessarily to disregard the reality expressed by the former image or concept.

By way of illustration, "omniscience" is the term by which Christians traditionally have expressed their faith in a God whose knowledge of things is wholly adequate; the concept itself, however, derives from alien philosophical cultures and carries meanings which are not as readily applicable in a Christian perspective as many have seemed to believe. Philosophically, the idea arises out of a theory of knowledge that supposes all adequate knowledge to be of actualities only; according to this view, undetermined possibilities cannot be "known." An omniscient being would be one who knows every actuality fully. But the kind of being to which "omniscience" came to be ascribed was *also* thought of as the all-sufficient ground of all things, without whom nothing could be what it is (or, in some forms of thought, could be at all). Once the two convictions are linked together, namely, that there is an all-sufficient source of things and that the knowledge possessed by that all-sufficient source is perfect knowledge of *actualities*, it becomes an easy matter to conclude that *only* actualities can be real. Otherwise, there would "be" a region of unactualized possibilities in some sense beyond the sovereign control of the all-sufficient One, a contradiction in terms. When such a pattern of thinking is integrated into an exposition of the Christian doctrine of God, unfortunate implications ensue for the understanding of time and history. Since upon this view past, present, and future must be known as actual by any being who knows all there is to be known, the future already must be actualized in the same way in which the past and present are actualized; the future is a fixed order into which all things move. The obvious difficulty with this postulate is that it collides with another major emphasis of faith, upon man's freedom; faith holds that the future depends in part upon how man exercises freedom in the present. If this latter be the case, the future *cannot* be determinately actualized and therefore *cannot* be of the same order as are the present and past. Traditionally, this internal inconsistency in the presentation of Christian faith has been countered by an adroit theological maneuver; a dubious distinction is posited between God's knowledge and his ordering, to permit the assertion that God can know the future without ordaining it. Thus, since things need not be viewed as foreordained, man in some sense still remains free for the future. But how can one be said to be free in *any* sense whose future is a given in God's knowing? Once the force of this question is felt, concept revision may appear highly desirable; what faith needs to say about the Transcendent Knower might better be said by means of concepts other than that of omniscience. The crucial observation, however, is that to disbelieve in divine omniscience is not to deny that there is a God whose knowledge of things is sufficient; it is simply to express doubt that the classical concept of omniscience adequately exhibits God's knowledge.

Often, this kind of disbelief among theologians is viewed as undermining the church's faith. But its aim really is to enhance the very possibility of faith—as may be the aim, by way of further example, of denying the virgin conception of Jesus, if what is meant is that the concept does not do justice to the concrete historicality of Jesus Christ witnessed to in the New Testament, however important it may be as a rudimentary statement of the later well-developed "two natures" doctrine of the Council of Chalcedon. There may be other and better ways to emphasize Christ's divinity than either of these formulations. Contemporary theology has entered a period of reconsidering the entire set of concepts by which the church traditionally sought to represent the reality to which faith owes its allegiance. Many theologians are haunted by grave doubts about the adequacy of the received tradition at its very foundation; as the first chapter endeavored to point out, it is highly problematic whether speech about God is any longer possible at all if governed by classical concepts. But what must not be overlooked in this frequently agonized discussion is that it has to do with the adequacy of theological concepts and not with the reality of faith itself.

The secular Christian's problem of unbelief arises whenever he finds it necessary to employ categories for interpreting his authentic contemporary experience which are not congruent with those he feels he ought to employ as a Christian. Though for integrity's sake he feels he must withhold assent to traditional Christian ways of speaking, he may not be abandoning faith as such. The difficulty he experiences is inability clearly to think through his situation of living in two worlds. He clearly disbelieves the conceptual framework of "Sunday school" faith. But he retains an interest in faith, nevertheless, and is profoundly disturbed that he cannot see how to develop that interest responsibly in a way which does justice to the best insights of his secular understanding. It will be presumed in the next chapter that there is nothing about secularity in itself which in principle makes a vital faith either impossible or inordinately difficult, whatever may be the actual feelings of specific believers. But it must be conceded that there persists intense conflict in contemporary understanding between secularity and traditional Christianity which man cannot abide indefinitely; one way or the other the conflict will be resolved, for human beings cannot live for very long or very fruitfully according to ways of conceiving reality which seem contradictory. The sectarian has already resolved the conflict by rejecting the positive possibilities of secularity. Others have given up the faith because they cannot find in the classical teachings of Christianity an intelligible and believable framework for interpreting present-day experience.

What is needed, therefore, is a careful consideration of the experience of faith underlying traditional Christianity in order to determine precisely how it is and is not incongruent with contemporary experience of the secular world. This must include a close look at faith's conceptualizing in the light of the reality which grounds it, in order to see how or whether its traditional concepts might be recast. If the outcome is to be salutary for the claims of faith, it will have to be the case that the realities undergirding the world views both of secularism and faith are commensurate, and that there is a way to express this compatibility adequately even if a wholesale revision of basic theological concepts turns out to be necessary. But there is good reason to be encouraged over the prospects of such an inquiry from the very outset; as has already been shown, prayer itself presupposes certain convictions about God which are not easily expressed in the received tradition, already requiring at several points a rejection of those classical concepts which accentuate God's holiness at the expense of his availability. Prayer already transcends orthodoxy as it penetrates more deeply into the ground of faith than many theological doctrines appear to do.

What then, specifically, is there about prayer which, when expressed conceptually, seems to conflict with secular man's experience? Fundamentally, the supposition that in this incomprehensibly large and impersonal universe transactions can and do take place between human beings and a suprahistorical, supranatural, personal Being, who can be present anywhere and at any time, and who from time to time intervenes to alter the uniform sequence of events within which human life comes to its fulfillment. Though divine intervention, as has been maintained previously, need not be understood as a disruption of the predictable order of nature, it is nevertheless alleged that God's involvement with persons demonstrably affects their capacities to persist faithfully, in times of trial and tribulation especially. All of the problems which contemporary man encounters in considering prayer as a suitable activity for him are centered in these underlying convictions, all of which are obviously indispensable to the practice of prayer. These convictions cannot be subject to reconceptualizing, or else the very possibility of prayer is undermined. But they cannot be believed readily, either. The task, therefore, must be to show that in the last analysis contemporary understanding does not preclude intelligent affirmation of just these beliefs.

For purposes of clarity, it may be helpful to distinguish the issues more precisely. The *first* difficulty is suggested by the notion that the universe at large is somehow supportive of human striving at its very foundation, a difficult matter for a scientifically informed person to entertain seriously. Modern science pictures the cosmos in terms of immense size and virtually unimaginable age, composed of billions of planets, on no one of which except earth is there as yet undeniable evidence of human life. Man appears to be alone in the universe, so far as is presently known. How, then, is it possible seriously to believe that the order of things comprises the habitation of human beings whose earnest pleas are dealt with creatively by a supremely personal Being who pervades the whole and transforms it, by his presence, into a neighborhood? One condition for serious prayer would seem to be *cosmological naïveté*.

The *second* difficulty which must be addressed arises from the concept of a God who is humanlike. There is nothing particularly new about this problem; from the outset, the more philosophically minded of the Western world have remained highly suspicious of the frank and sometimes crass anthropomorphism of biblical literature and pious testimony. But the suspicions are peculiarly widespread in the present era, given secular man's understanding of a universe which cannot in principle accommodate the hypothesis that *any* being could be transported with infinite speed to be present anywhere according to his good pleasure, much less a large humanlike being; does not the absolutely limiting condition of the finite speed of light call seriously into question that any being could be present anywhere upon a mere prayerful sigh's notice? This difficulty, already referred to in the first chapter in a different context, can be labeled *anthropomorphism*.

The *final* difficulty is with the concept of events altered by divine decree. This, too, is not a new problem, but it has become an especially serious one recently, given secular man's understanding of things. The difficulty is that of *interventionism*. Softened though the previously elaborated interventionist view is over that of medieval Christianity, which could depict miracles transpiring seemingly everywhere in both history and nature, unless some limited form of interventionism is defensible in the light of man's best understanding of things, petitionary and intercessory prayer can make no sense.

Properly to deal with these issues requires elaborating in some detail the serious possibility of *another* way of explaining reality, that which faith always has sought to embody. But throughout any such analysis, one needs to face unflinchingly the possibility that to pray at all is to contradict all that he is to regard as reliable knowledge of things generally. Only by taking full notice of how secular man has come to dismiss as incredible any form of cosmological naïveté, anthropomorphism, and interventionism can prayer genuinely appear as a possibility for him. For only then can it be determined whether or not his dismissals are adequately grounded. This will be one of the major tasks of the final chapter.

CHAPTER 4

GOD IN A SECULAR WORLD

The preceding chapters have attempted to show that prayer is possible only for those who can sustain three basic convictions: (1) that the whole of reality is conducive to the actualization of distinctively human possibilities (cosmological naïveté); (2) that man's central position in the universe is ensured by the purposing of a supremely personal creator of the whole (anthropomorphism); and (3) that God is active in his created order, constantly providing all that is required to enhance human existence (interventionism). Further, it was argued that unless these convictions also represent what truly is the case, then the essence of prayer, earnest petitions and intercessions before One believed capable both of hearing and responding effectively to them, cannot make sense. Finally, the thesis was advanced that it is just these convictions which are so difficult for secular believers to affirm.

What remains, for this concluding chapter, is to establish the plausibility of prayer's perspective on reality. Beginning with a reconsideration of how the God of faith should and should not be represented in language, the chapter will then seek to exhibit the congruity between an *adequate* conceptualization of God and that understanding of reality which is determinative for secular consciousness. To put the matter more specifically still: The aim is to exhibit the possibility of prayer in a secular world by showing how a truly faithful representation of God is compatible with an uncompromisingly secular view of reality.

It will be argued that the difficulties about Christian faith which affect the intensity of prayer arise from a certain way of clarifying belief intellectually but are not present at the level of belief itself. It has always been the case that those who believe without understanding remain insulated from many of the corrosive effects of intellectual endeavor upon devotional life. But "simple" faith of this sort is merely simplistic or simpleminded; blatantly anti-intellectual to the core, it ought not to command serious attention by anyone. Its pervasiveness, however, points to an important feature of faith itself: its power to determine the quality of one's life independently of his interpreting it. Many live laudatory lives of loving God and neighbor without fully comprehending what they are about and why they do the worthy things they do. For many genuine believers, faith is a knowing *how* which never becomes a knowing *that*. What this suggests is that whenever faith suffers as a result of its being interpreted, it is the peculiar terminology of the interpretation which is at fault. By searching out the temporarily obscured faith underlying the questionable interpretation, it may be possible in all cases to reduce the force of a particular doubt wrongly believed to pertain to faith itself.

The thesis now to be advanced is that the peculiar problems accompanying secular Christians' believing in God are germane only to certain and particular characterizations of God which do not in fact exhibit clearly the reality to which faith witnesses. Following a definition of what must be fundamental in any adequate representation of God, and then of what particular conceptualization of God has made prayer so difficult to entertain seriously, the chapter will explore faith's foundational experience of God, that which at once underlies and negates every troublesome and inadequate representation of God. The vital center of faith has sustained and will continue to sustain the life of prayer, in spite of every intellectual dilemma haunting thoughtful men and women in the contemporary secular world. In the recovery of that vital center, the possibility of prayer impinges anew upon the lives of secular believers.

CREATION FAITH
AND ITS MISUNDERSTANDING

To bring clearly into view the divine Being to whom prayer properly is addressed, Christian faith always and rightly has turned to Jesus Christ, who is believed uniquely to qualify man's understanding of God. However, the way in which God is disclosed in Jesus is incomprehensible apart from the history in which Jesus was a participant. Jesus' heavenly Father was none other than Abraham's also, the same Lord who freed the Jews from slavery in Egypt and who challenged continually his covenant community to be a light to the nations. But in all of his dealings with man, God is understood fundamentally as the *source of all things*. Whether it is Abraham, Moses, Isaiah, or Jesus himself speaking, the gracious God spoken of is the all-sovereign creator and sustainer of the world. In this understanding of God, Jesus also stood. He, too, conceived of God primarily by reference to all that God is doing in the world of which he is the maker. Hence, Christian faith has sought to exhibit God by first learning to look upon each finite being, and the totality of finite beings, *sacramentally*, as visible signs pointing toward and partly embodying their single source.

Along with its sacramental understanding of the world,

114

however, creation faith also cautions against representing God after the fashion of other beings, for example, as if he were merely alongside the beings of the world he has created. As the transcendent source of the entire order of being, God's own being must be supposed utterly different in kind from that of any being he creates. These polar emphases constitute many of the seemingly strange features of traditional language about God. On the one hand, believers speak about God in ways analogous to their speech about the created order, usually on the ground that God, in creating the finite order, has filled it with evidences of his handiwork which can be taken as symbols of his own being. On the other hand, every believer is taught that all such analogies finally break down, because God, as the transcendent source of all there is, does not (and perhaps cannot) himself share any feature in common with the world he creates. For if his being were in any way akin to anything in the created order, that order itself would be divine. In light of these and similar considerations, the doctrine of the incarnation, affirming the full entrance into the finite order of One who is in no way like unto finite beings, is alleged to be a sheer paradox, wholly beyond human understanding.

Creation faith, which Jesus also shared, thus has posed two kinds of grievous difficulties for Christian understanding in every generation. The first arises whenever God's unlikeness to his creation (transcendence) is stressed. To say that God is very different from his creation is to border on vacuity. To say, with no small part of the tradition, that God is a being *infinitely* different from anything human beings can experience and know is to have become vacuous utterly; such language reduces to a potentially infinite number of statements about what God is not, which cannot ever yield even one positive statement about what God is. However pious the motivation may be for speaking of God in this way, there is no discernible difference between believing thusly and believing in no God at all; neither belief affirms the availability of the transcendent source of all being to those who call upon him. A God who is wholly other is dead, so far as faith is concerned.

The second difficulty accompanies the contrasting emphasis: Stressing God's likeness to his creation, by virtue of his being its source, frequently leads to inappropriate statements about him, incongruous with the ways in which believers are taught to address God respectfully as the holy Source of life. Every affirmation of the likeness of God to the beings of which he is the source verges upon representing God inadequately as another being among the beings in the world—the most real, powerful, and worthy being, to be sure, but nevertheless *a* being, an entity among other entities, an object among other objects. For example, the righteousness of God is often expressed, according to such a way of speaking, by the image of an implacable judge, firmly ensconced upon a throne, surrounded by messengers awaiting his command to deliver his sovereign decrees. Such *objectifying* thinking—that is, thinking which "brings God down to the object world"—cannot generate adequate symbols for God's holiness.

To put the dilemma in the terminology used in previous chapters: The unity of God's holiness and accessibility is extraordinarily difficult and perhaps impossible to conceive in relationship with the created order. *To emphasize God's holiness seems to empty faith statements of all content, and to emphasize accessibility seems to achieve a content quite incommensurate with devotion to an all-worthy source of all there is.*

Responsible thinking about this dilemma cannot take place unless it begins by noting how very strange it is that every effort to think about God understandingly should have given rise to these difficulties. For the difficulties do not appear troublesome at the primary level of faith. Though God does indeed come to man as the Holy One (i.e., Isaiah 6:1-5), man's response to the encounter rarely is articulated in a conception of God as *wholly* transcendent. Faith views God as at least sufficiently like man to hear and answer man's prayers, and without compromising his holiness. Further, faith repeatedly has overcome the temptation to think of finite reality as *un*godly, somehow incapable of "bearing" the divine presence. No matter how "fallen" mankind and the cosmos once may have been, the created order cannot now be utterly estranged from its ground; for this very fallen world, God's own son died. The likeness of being between God and his creation, presupposed in every serious act of prayer, is disclosed in the gracious redemption of the world by God himself.

In spite of faith's own clarity about these matters, however, the *doctrine* of God as creator seems always to be expressed in language which is either vacuous or inappropriate or both. Though every such doctrine seeks to avoid each kind of danger, none has succeeded. Usually, the failure is "justified" by appealing to the divine transcendence itself, which, it is then alleged, makes all human speech about God problematic. But upon this account, God's availability has been lost sight of. For if finite creatures, by virtue of their finitude and/or fallenness, cannot presume to say anything true about the Most Holy One, how can they ever be confident about the accessibility of that Holy One?

The conclusion which might be drawn from this observation is that faith better understands divine matters *without* the aid of theological doctrines. Tempting as the hypothesis is, however, it finally will not do, if for no other reason than that a faithful community will produce doctrines, whether it wishes to do so or not; it is in the very nature of faith to demand the kind of understanding

117

which doctrines and theologians who produce them attempt to articulate. Even when certain ways of theologizing about God exacerbate the difficulties of being faithful, the theological enterprise itself remains indispensable. Faith arises out of events of divine-human encounter charged with such intensity as to command the participants' attention wholly. The import of such events for the whole of life is not immediately evident in the events themselves; only in the calm following the storm, so to speak, can the essential work begin of reflecting upon what has transpired. Theology is essentially that faithful act of reflection, a gathering and careful considering of the prior experiences of faith, which seeks their deeper significance for the tonality and style of man's entire life. Faith cannot do without such reflection. But, as now should be evident, the advantages gained are not without their accompanying cost. Clarification often transforms the original meanings of what is clarified into meaning complexes that are not faith's own. Why is this so?

Primarily, because every clarifying act is achieved through imposing upon the experience of revelatory events the presuppositions and principles by which experience as a whole is interpreted in the cultural milieu generally. In Christian theology, that which is imposed is for the most part a pattern of thinking which was founded by the ancient Greek philosophers and perfected with the rise of modern science. In order to show how the whole of human experience is illumined by the gospel of Jesus Christ, the church found it necessary to adopt that conceptual scheme by means of which Western experience was interpreted generally. The results generally were salutary, in the sense that the doctrinal teachings which ensued genuinely clarified faith for many who were dubious as to its possibilities. But the price paid was the importation of metaphysical dilemmas into the very exposition of Christian faith. The way in which creation faith becomes intellectually problematic when expressed according to this pattern of interpreting experience now must be looked at in greater detail, with particular import for belief in a God who hears and answers prayers.

When the church sought to examine carefully its belief in God as creator, and to bring to clear expression what is implied in affirming a single transcendent source of all things, it made use of a widely prevalent understanding, derived from Greek metaphysics, of what *world*-as-such is. According to that understanding, by "world" is meant a *totality* of *things* or *objects.* Each thing/object is conceived of as possessing three primary characteristics. The first is *spatial and temporal location,* a calculable position in space and time. Each thing in part *is* its relation to every other thing specified by a set of spatial and temporal coordinates. Crucial to this conception is that no more than one thing can occupy the same spatiotemporal position; each thing is measurably at a distance from every other thing. Contemporary scientific thinking reluctantly concludes that, in the totality, some things are so distant from one another that apparently they cannot interact at all. As has been suggested previously, upon such a view it is difficult to conceive of God acting simultaneously in response to different prayerful addresses, especially if those addresses generate in different regions of the universe. The second characteristic is *causal determination,* acting upon other beings, and being acted upon by them, in ways governed by causal laws. Two conceptions of the world's causal structure have been advanced within this single framework of thought. Some have held that the causal principles are embedded within the very being of each thing, that the totality of things is a harmonious and self-sufficient whole wherein from all eternity each thing acts and is acted upon according to determinants internal to its very essence. Others have held the view, upon which classical theology depends, that causal connections between things are governed by laws imposed by something external both to each thing and to the totality itself. Upon this latter conception, God as creator means God as ultimate cause of that totality whose essence includes causal structure. The third characteristic is *interiority,* an essence undetermined by its relationships with other things. While everything interacts with other things in a spatiotemporal system of causal determination, no thing truly can *be* unless also it "is" something which remains what it is through its subjection to causal determination. Each thing is independent of, as well as dependent upon, its relationships with other things.

It should be evident immediately that this conception of what world is as such affirms a sharp distinction between things and the beings who *know* of things; "things known" and "knowers" represent two radically different orders of being. How the totality of things can include beings seemingly so different in kind from the things they know is one of the persisting questions which haunts the Greek view of "world." The tragic picture is of conscious beings transcending while remaining dependent upon a thing-world whose nurture is never wholly trustworthy. How consciousness is at all in that thing-world remains a fascinating but ineluctable mystery.

Whatever their origin, conscious beings attuned to all that can be known will experience the thing-world in one of three ways: as a threat to selves, as malleable to selves' designs, or as merely impervious to consciousness, something one is brought up against and which remains there, no matter what. Though contemporary man often brazenly posits the plasticity of the thing-world to his own creativity, it is the last idea which really dominates his thinking. In moments of sobriety and candor contemporary man finds himself conceding that he lives in a universe neither hostile to him nor open to his purposing, but rather in a totality careless of his hopes and longings, within which his little life is merely the strangest of accidents. That things are conceived of as occupying a different order of being from that of selves will have serious implications for every attempt to conceive of God as creator in terms of creator of a *thing*-world.

But before this matter can be dealt with directly, some observations must be made about the relationship of this kind of thinking in general to classical theological thinking about God. Given the above-defined characteristics of the being of *things,* what is to be said about the being of God when God is conceived as the *source* of all things? Certain features of the thing-world do suggest a likeness of being between worldly things and God. God can be said to be thinglike in at least two senses: as an agent acting upon other things as cause to effect, and in his self-identity by virtue of an essence which remains eternally unaffected by any and all relationships to anything else. By objectifying faith's experience of God in only these two ways, classical theological thinking generated the doctrine that creation itself is an act of grace by an absolutely self-sufficient being whose interiority is in no way altered by his creating *any* world, much less *this* one.

However enticing it may be to think about both the world and God in *thing* terms, however, there are good reasons for believing it is wholly inappropriate to do so. Even a cursory examination of what believers also mean by "God" should make plain that objectifying representations cannot do justice to the One who elicits man's faith. In the first place, unlike things, God is said not to have either spatial or temporal location; the church has taught, rightly, that God cannot be defined by reference to any set of spatial or temporal coordinates. God is omnipresent; that is, he can be anywhere or everywhere, at his own choosing. Second, unlike things, God is said never to be acted upon by anything (or anyone) other than himself; though he himself acts upon other beings, no other being can impinge upon God so as to bring about any significant alteration in the divine life. (It is both fitting and appropriate, in the light of previous considerations, to underline again how puzzling is this feature of the classical doctrine of God: It is impossible to take petitionary and intercessory prayer seriously if one believes also that God cannot be influenced to do what he has not previously decided to do. Thus, it is difficult in the extreme to understand the time-honored support for the traditional doctrine of God's unchangeableness.) Third and most importantly, biblical images converge in their representation of God as selflike rather than thinglike. Thus, it is not only *logically* inappropriate to think about God as thinglike, it is *religiously* inappropriate as well; worship is of a conscious and caring person, not of a causal agent. (It might also be said, with many contemporary theologians, that it is inappropriate to speak of God as thinglike because the world view which results is no longer credible. No one, it is said, any longer *experiences* invasions into the thing-world of a divine being who directly influences the course of events in that thing-world; those who say otherwise are regarded by thoughtful people as deluded. Whoever thinks that there are divine things operative in the causal order, appearing in particular spaces and times to work their will and then withdrawing, simply fails to comprehend adequately how the experienced world "really" is structured.)

God's being cannot be thought of, then, as analogous with that of things in a thing-world. The reason most frequently advanced for drawing this conclusion, as noted previously but in a different context, is that God is the transcendent source *of* that thing-world. But this latter proposition is also problematic in the extreme, for there is no clear meaning conceivable for the idea upon which it rests: namely, the idea of "source of all things." The very concept of "source" derives its meaning only *from* and *within* a thing-world; as such, it cannot apply in the same sense *to* that thing-world as a totality. Human beings experience "origination" as the emergence of things within some totality, by rearrangement of constituent ingredients in that totality. Their concepts expressing interactions *between* things, then, cannot apply to the origination of the totality *of* things without vacuity resulting. Logically speaking, to ask about the *source* of *everything* is to misapply categories of thinking, as in the seemingly legitimate but actually nonsensical question, "What is the color of an electron?" On this latter example, given that color, by definition, is a quality of one's visual experiences of phenomena, the term color cannot apply to anything which by nature is not visible, such as electrons, curved space, or $\sqrt{1}$. If man has no experience at all of the production of *the* totality of things, he does not speak intelligibly when he affirms God to be the transcendent source of all things.

In sum, creation faith comes to theological expression within a conceptual framework which in itself can provide an understanding neither of the distinctive being of God nor of the way in which a *totality* of things could come into being as a creative act of God. Whenever "world" is taken to mean "totality of things," in the senses just enumerated, it can make no sense whatever to speak either of God as the source of that world or of that world's constituents as bearing nothing less than sacramental significance. *Objectifying* thinking, whether in its metaphysical or in its scientific form, cannot do justice to the very creation faith which for centuries the church has employed it to interpret.

Before attempting an alternative conceptualization of creation faith, however, some remarks are in order about the significance of objectifying thinking for understanding experience generally. It cannot be denied that objectifying thinking has aided immeasurably in man's monumental effort to overcome his primitive disposition to think of

123

all beings as ensouled (animism). That reality includes things as well as souls is a liberating discovery. One is spared the anxieties accompanying the belief that everything one encounters is alive. But in transforming *all* appearances into appearances of *objects* rather than of *conscious centers,* objectifying thinking makes reality appear to be an encompassing order in which consciousness is merely an enigma. By so doing, it increases the likelihood that those same creatures it liberates from animism will avoid fully confronting both the threat and the promise of *selfhood.* The awesome burden of becoming, self-consciously, a person is easily minimized if one is encouraged to look upon himself and others as things in a thing-world. Everyone finds it is less intimidating to be a thing than to be a self, to let himself be affected by everything else according to externally imposed principles of interaction, over which he has no control, rather than to enter into mutually supportive relationships with other selves by lovingly assuming responsibility for his impact upon them. For human beings it is always possible to choose a careless existence, to enjoy stimulation by everything else without moral investment in the responsibility of being a caring stimulator. Objectifying thinking enhances the possibility of making such a choice.

Perhaps this is the reason why objectifying language pervades even the utterances of faith. Believers, too, participate wholly in the human condition. And though their faith promises liberation from its destructive burden, they too seek to deny their richest possibilities. Intimidated by being destined for personal relationships with each other and with their eminently personal creator, they evade God's call to responsible selfhood by portraying objectifyingly God's interaction with the created order. The faith which results calls only for awed acknowledgment of wonders not possible for human beings, unimaginable feats of causal efficacy: stopping the earth's rotation on its axis, enabling a man to walk on water, ascending through earth's atmosphere without benefit of rocket boosters, and so on, ad infinitum. When God is so conceived as analogous to things in a thing-world, the finality of the thing-world is assured. Man is no longer burdened with the possibility of a self-world disclosed from "beyond."

However threatening may be the idea of deobjectifying the language of faith for many believers, that for which the term stands is altogether crucial for any adequate portrayal of the God who does indeed disclose himself to faithful creatures. Only by deobjectifying (variously termed "existentializing" or "demythologizing") the traditional understanding of God as source of all there is, can one hope to perceive that the genuine point of encounter between God and man is in the dimension of selfhood and personhood. Deobjectifying is not called for primarily as a way of speaking more adequately about God. Faith already includes the assurance that God will not leave his people without a witness to him; there never has been cause for inordinate preoccupation with discovering on one's own the proper way to speak about God. Rather, deobjectifying is indispensable because it reopens the possibility that belief in God can illumine man's destiny in a community of conscious selves, transforming his persistent preoccupation with the thing-world into a new vision of the reality which encompasses him. The positive form which such deobjectifying is to take will be examined now in greater detail.

GOD AND HUMAN HOPING

Christian faith is primarily an expression of *human self-understanding*. Its language is about neither God, in himself, nor about the ways in which events transpire in the thing-world. It is not *the Truth* about ultimate reality although it includes true statements about the Ultimate. And it is not a superior "science," although it includes a perspective on the natural order which sees meaning and purpose where the scientist frequently can see none. Faith has to do, primarily though never exclusively, with man's innermost being, individual and communal; it expresses one understanding of the human situation in the order of being as a whole, one way of perceiving the human environing world. It is an affective response to the whole of a perceived environment, a total state of mind at a particular moment toward the entire contents of consciousness. Qualifying the whole of consciousness, faith encompasses in a unity the emotions, will, and intellect. Its comprehensibility derives from the power of its mood to permeate the cognitive activities of discernment and judgment. The possibility of understanding faith at all derives from the fact that in every state of mind there is a cognitive dimension awaiting clarification, those acts of cognition which seek to discern what had elicited its all-encompassing state of mind.

Because faith *must* clarify to itself the *reality* of that which has evoked it, its theologies cannot avoid becoming metaphysical in character. The problem with classical Christian theology is not that it engaged in metaphysics at all but that it did not adequately envision the possibility that there is more than one theory of reality in accordance with which it could work out adequately faith's own understanding of God as the *sustaining power of selfhood*. That theology resembles abstract metaphysical thinking frequently leads believers and nonbelievers alike to the mistaken view that faith itself is primarily descriptive of divine reality rather than expressive of man's response in trust to that divine reality, whose disclosures always remain surrounded by impenetrable mystery.

For example, since the late sixteenth century (and rarely if ever before), many have taken it as a life-or-

126

death matter that the church uphold the scriptures as a deposit of literally true statements about God and his doings in the world, inerrant and exhaustive of the divine self-disclosures. Not only does thinking of this sort wrongly construe the basic form of scriptural language, it goes on to interpret the form by those categories which facilitate interpretation of experience in a thing-world. The kinds of statements frequently alleged to be infallibly true in the Bible are those which portray reality as an object-world presided over by an all-sovereign Super-Thing. Narrations of miraculous occurrences in violation of physical laws usually constitute the test case for the "inerrancy" doctrine; unless one holds these narrations to be literally true, so the argument goes, the very reliability of God's Word is compromised. In spite of Jesus' own protestations to the contrary, many of his most devoted followers, from his day to the present, look upon him as a miracle worker, constantly insinuating himself into the natural order for the sake of effecting extraordinary testimonies to his transcendent power. Without calling into question the *authority* of the scriptures, it nevertheless must be conceded that much of its objectifying language simply is incredible for those who take secular understanding seriously. Secular believers no longer can appreciate a faith which constantly expects cosmic invasions by semidivine beings. They *can* appreciate interpreting the Christian faith as human self-understanding in response to a caring Presence. While contemporary hearers of the gospel cannot suppose seriously that anyone could still a storm through the sound of his voice, they have experienced from the depths what it is like to be fearful of the world and to be claimed by another self in that world so intensely that he would bring threatening weather immediately to a halt, if he could, in order to help that other overcome his dread.

Faith, then, intends not so much to describe that which

it sees as to articulate believers' moods, within which their faith as the *response* to what is seen is nourished. The dominant characteristic of the mood which is faith is *hopefulness*. That which faith has discerned, which creates the mood of hope, is the possibility that *every believer has a significant future*. Faith is the response to the discernment that all of the enhancing experiences of human life may persist, that their destiny may be something other than being extinguished in endless interactions between *things*. The possibility of an afterlife, of immortality, is a necessary implication of wholeheartedly anticipating any sort of significant future. Faith begins with the acknowledgment that man's years are "three score and ten" but proceeds immediately to affirm ultimate significance about these temporal limitations, all appearances to the contrary notwithstanding. In its maturing, faith increasingly projects the possibility of an *indefinitely* extended future, rightly discerning that if there is significance to man's future in a qualitative sense, that very significance is heightened to the extent that it is also experienced over the greatest possible time. It is difficult to understand how one could feel a part of the historic Christian faith and yet dismiss as unnecessary any belief in the afterlife. The symbols of resurrection and eternality are too pervasive to be dismissed and too powerful to be translated into other terms, such as through projecting one's immortality in the fond memories of others, either other human beings' or God's. Hope does not envision man's future merely objectifyingly, as bare persistence at a particular spatiotemporal location. Its concern is that the most *enriching* human experiences shall abide, though reality threatens at every moment to annul them. Faith knows that hopefulness is possible always and only because of the sufficiency of One who sustains the future of all worlds, present and yet to come.

To believe in God, then, is to deny that reality is either

hostile or neutral to the human future. It is to deny that reality is exclusively a thing-world to be feared, exploited, or merely wondered at. To believe in God is to believe that each human being has a significant future and that reality itself supports that future. Both sheer longing and resolute expectation express the inner dynamic of faith. Sometimes a faithful person reckons his future only wistfully, with a yearning bordering on desperation. On other occasions his mood shifts; he regains confidence about that future. Sometimes he wonders if hoping is not blind. At other times he feels an unconquerable assurance that his hopes are reality-oriented after all. Throughout, however, the state of mind which is faith points beyond every conscious being's own aspirations to transcendent reality itself. Faith is a confrontation with the future as God's own bestowal of possibility. It is not wistfulness unsupported by any experience of divine presence. No one can yearn, even pathetically, for a future that he *knows* is not to be his. One who concludes that there are no good grounds for being hopeful about the future, that the so-called discernments of faith are merely childlike fantasies to be set aside in the normal course of maturation, has already abandoned faith as a possibility for him. Genuine faith always refers to something beyond man which actively occasions hope, however doubt-ridden faith also becomes from time to time. Faith is not unctuous speech about man which deludes people into supposing falsely that there is a God.

But what kind of discernment sustains the mood of faith in spite of every doubt human beings have experienced through the centuries? What is the content of that primal understanding of reality which enables human beings to be affirmative about their own prospects, even and especially for the distant future, in spite of all evidence to the contrary which points to the inevitable extinction of human life in the universe? The answer to this question

129

will provide a way of conceiving God which is a genuine alternative to that of objectifying thinking. It will make plausible, as objectifying thinking cannot, believing in a God to whom one could pray.

The primal self-understanding of men and women of faith is that the human self and its environing world together have a significant future grounded in the order of being itself. Abstractly put, the understanding which is expressed in anticipating a significant future is the understanding of a being conscious of itself as a concentration of being in a world other than itself, a gathering and focusing of being within a wider world upon which one is dependent and from which one also is free. In order to bring out the concrete character of this primal act of understanding, the components of this complex statement must be examined more closely, under the separate headings, respectively, of "worldedness" and "centeredness." The meaning of "God" will be exhibited as that which faith discerns to be the ground both of self's worldedness and centeredness. The thesis is that faith is the self-conscious act of a being who is both centered and worlded (as opposed to "worldly"; "worldliness" carries too many lingering and negatively charged meanings to be helpful any longer in serious theological discussion). Faith is possible at all only to self-conscious beings who have discovered themselves as centered in an environment in specific ways; its career is an integral feature of a more inclusive process of developing self-consciousness through which human beings grow in their awareness of both their supportive environment and their inner integrity unassailed by the threatening aspects of that environment. As in the development of self-consciousness generally, faith also begins with the awareness of worldedness and only gradually achieves awareness of centeredness. One first assumes prescribed roles and fulfills partly the expectations of those imposing them; only then does he usually begin to wrest his own selfhood from the conditioning by "those others." By clarifying both worldedness and centeredness, then, the foundations of hoping should become comprehensible and, with them, the God upon whose promises one rests every hope. But faith, as the act of trusting that "all will be well," is comprehensible *only* in the light shining from this wider horizon of human experiencing: from a world, and from a center of being in that world.

WORLDEDNESS

By "world" is meant a perceived totality of things and relations whose *being* is the *import* they bear for the *percipient's welfare*. It includes the totality of appearances which stimulate the sensoria, all that is and can be taken note of by conscious beings. The term, then, derives from an examination of the contents of conscious activities and states and is not to be understood in the ordinary sense, geographically. *Self*-consciouness depends upon the prior consciousness of a world within which one "is" *as* a self. One discovers his own being as a self, in that wider world, primarily through learning to distinguish from the plethora of appearances impinging upon his senses, centers of being which are both nonconscious and conscious (usually in this order). Self-consciousness becomes possible when a sentient creature is so affected by such appearances that it begins to reflect upon the very experiencing of them; by means of such reflection, one discovers *oneself* in the experiencing of them.

The altogether crucial observation about this foundational level of experiencing is that *that which appears is not adequately described as things in a totality*. Rather, what first impinges upon a receptive and conscious being is encountered as either threatening to or supportive of the percipient. To put the point in the strongest possible way:

131

What first appears is *essentially* either a threatening or a supportive being. A pertinent illustration is the behavior of newborns. The first month of life seems to indicate that the kind of reality which first impinges upon consciousness is the reality of *threatening* beings. However, an infant soon begins to differentiate, within the totality, appearances of beings which nurture and sustain from appearances of beings which loom ominously: for example, the appearance of a nipple from the appearance of spacious walls which do not enclose snugly. As he learns to make these kinds of distinctions, the infant also becomes aware, in a rudimentary way, of himself as a center of being *to whom* appearances are of both welcome and dangerous beings. But every appearance is of a being whose essence is always and entirely its value to himself; to the infant, every being *is* either encouragement or intimidation, promise or threat. What the example is intended to show is that the primary experience of "world" for self-conscious beings is not that of a totality of things which are merely spatially and temporally extended, causally connected, and which are what they are independently of their effects upon any conscious being whatever. Rather, self-conscious beings experience their environing world initially and most fundamentally as a matrix of values and not as a totality of things or objects. All beings are encountered primordially in the mode of their *mattering to.* They *are* the way they matter to someone; they *are* the significance they hold for their perceivers' welfare; they *are* their invitingness or their forbiddingness.

Most of the difficulties secular believers experience with prayer arise from a view of reality framed in objectifying terms, whose central conviction is that what truly is is impervious to human hoping and, indeed, impervious to conscious beings as such, whether hopeful or otherwise. Much of the force of this conviction derives from its being taken as an insight of "common sense" which is uniformly confirmed by the modern scientific world picture. This supposedly commonsense distinction, however, between things existing independently of their being perceived by anyone, and the representations of those things in images or concepts, is an extraordinarily sophisticated philosophical construction of "world." The commonsense view actually is closer to that of the newborn, perceiving other beings unashamedly in terms of their positive or negative impact. Common sense grows in understanding its world largely through the trial-and-error procedure of judging whether various appearances *in fact* are of either threatening or supportive beings; but even in its maturity it is not interested in things in themselves, independently of their positive or negative import in experience. Primary knowledge is of what is to be embraced and of what must be avoided from the plethora of appearances which continually intrude into consciouness.

In seeking to reopen the possibility of prayer for secular believers, the first step is to note how closely the childlike naïveté of prayer is related to the most primitive and determinative way of experiencing reality. The supposed "cosmological naïveté" of prayer's world view may be erroneous, but it is *not* naïve; it rather expresses a foundational way of interpreting all appearances. The primal encounter between a self-conscious being and his world is encounter with a bewildering array of appearances which first and fundamentally are distinguished in terms of "supportive" and "threatening." It becomes possible to regard any of these as appearances of "things" *only* when their value as either support or threat is unclear. Only when one feels uncertainty about whether what now appears before him should be greeted warmly or retreated from hostilely can the process of objectifying thinking commence. Objectifying (or "thingifying") the content of appearances does not occur until there is some disruption in one's prior and primal relationships with reality; only then do self-conscious beings begin to distance themselves from the totality of appearances with which they had been more or less involved in order to look *at,* rather than to do *with,* the representations of those appearances in thought. Then and only then does thinking render the totality of appearances objective, to one whose state of mind now is one of cultivated indifference, strictly speaking of *un-care* (*a-pathos*). The aim now becomes seeing what is "out there" in itself, independently of any prior value(s) the thing seen may have held for a percipient.

The perenniality of such objectifying thinking points to the fact that disruptions in one's primal world relationships are unavoidable. For example, one cannot readily escape experiences such as the death of a pet. By and large, a "pet" *is* what it allows its master to do with it, as the term itself expresses. But pets frequently die unexpectedly, and when they do the master's primal relationship with a being whose essence *is* pet is broken; it is now possible, and indeed mandatory, for him to regard the pet's appearance totally differently. Once a value-laden being, the pet appears now, as it lies on the street, having been run down by a vagrant automobile, as a "corpse," a mere corporeal thing. The capacity to regard the animal thusly in such a situation is precisely that which underlies all objectifying thinking; whether in the form of metaphysics or science, objectifying thought exhibits the universal possibility for any and all appearances of being experienced merely as that of a corporeal thing and not as of a "snuggly." Tragic events, which occur predictably even if not necessarily, alter the stance that one takes toward any appearance. When the *primal* standpoint gives way to the *objective,* the hypothesis is suggested that reality itself may be of a different order altogether than the one in which all things are at all insofar as they bear import for self-conscious beings. When, for whatever reason, the value of any appearance becomes ambiguous for one's own well-being, the process begins which culminates in a thinking about every appearance as the appearance as of a *thing*.

Objectifying thinking, then, is derivative thinking, arising *only* when the primal relationships between self and world are temporarily and tragically disrupted. *At such times,* however, it may well be indispensable. It is frequently useful to "thingify" an appearance in order to restore its original value, if at all possible. For example, when one's hammer breaks, it is helpful to be able to thingify in thought the appearance of what previously he had been using in an unthinking manner to fashion something desirable, whether the restoration of a broken shingle or the creation of a masterpiece in bronze. He looks *at* the hammer in another way in order to get into a position to retrieve it; by relating to it altogether differently even if temporarily, he is able to put it back together again properly as an extension of his hand. There is great value in engaging in the kind of objectifying thinking which Greek metaphysics and modern science bring to utmost clarity, as long as objectifying the totality of appearances is not at the expense of that more basic value-world which constitutes man's primary world orientation. But Western thought has not succeeded very often in employing objectifying thinking in proper perspective. As has been argued previously in other terms, many of the basic concepts of objectifying thinking have served to increase man's forgetfulness of his primary relationship with reality. To illustrate in another context, Western metaphysics is an extended elaboration of the concept of substance, whose every specification implies an order of being radically other than that of the world in which conscious beings live. Early in the development of Greek thought substance came to be understood as that which is, above all, impervious to the self-world; "substance" is that which is and will be, whether there are any selves conscious of it at all. Given that kind of hegemony, it was frequently supposed, human life is best lived out in adaptation to the unalterable features of the substance-world within which conscious beings temporarily thrive. While substance may be neither threatening to nor supportive of man, its *neutrality* dictates that it can never adapt to man; thus man must adapt his ways to a permanently delimited order of substances and their interrelations.

Contrariwise, however, what should have been obvious long ago is that the very neutrality which a substance-world supposedly represents is *not* a mode of being independent of human judgments about its value. Neutrality itself is a value, whose sole meaning has to do with the effects upon conscious beings of other perceived beings. To experience another as neutral to one's own welfare is to experience that other as a value. Substance thinking has led many falsely to believe in a world of things whose defining characteristics are independent of any human experience. This is a profoundly mistaken view, however, because the very concept of substance can be entertained at all only when consciousness is disrupted at its more basic level. Any appearance to which man is truly related *is* its *worth,* to the self-conscious beings who either experience or assign that worth; it *is* at all insofar as it is either threatening to or supportive of centered beings. It is in this kind of "world" that selves truly exist. And it is about such a "world" that selves truly pray.

CENTEREDNESS

The centered self is, in its centeredness, a concentration of desire; the integrative experiences of self-conscious beings, by which they are gathered as centers of determinate being in their own right, are of desires and their satisfaction or nonsatisfaction. It is by reference to the experience of desire and its satisfaction that valuing terms, most especially "good" and "evil," function to organize all other experiences according to a scale of ascending and descending worth. The worth of any experience is the degree to which it achieves satisfaction of some desire. More precisely, what is valuable for its own sake, *intrinsic* value, is any experience of satisfied desire. And correlatively, disvalue is the absence of such satisfaction; "evil" is the frustration of some desire. So defined, evil seems a necessary feature of human existence. Present desire often goes unsatisfied for the sake of maximizing satisfying experiences in the future. And in many cases, the satisfaction of one desire requires frustrating another; for example, companionship is often traded for fame. In every instance, however, evil has to do only with the frustration of desire; events transpiring independently of any effect upon conscious creatures of desire are in the strictest possible sense "beyond good and evil." To illustrate, the opening of the San Andreas fault would be evil only if someone bemoans the ensuing destruction; the evil of an earthquake consists in the quality of experiences it generates and not in the mere alteration of topography. If the good for its own sake is the satisfaction of desire, then whatever contributes to the satisfaction of desire, whether things, persons, or situations, is good instrumentally, as a means to achieving what is good in itself.

Upon this view of selfhood, as the organizing of experience for the sake of maximizing satisfaction, there are as many ways of organizing experience as there are scales of value expressing different specifications of *which* experiences exhibit most completely the satisfaction of man's desires. Faith, insofar as it is held to by a centered self-conscious being, exhibits one kind of discernment about those values most worth pursuing. It is that the most satisfying kinds of experiences are those shared with other self-conscious beings voluntarily assembled and mutually committed to the well-being of everyone assembled. Faith calls every human being to life in a community, out of its conviction that the satisfaction of every human desire is best achieved when self-conscious beings pledge themselves to one another and to a higher cause which the whole community is to serve. Such loyalties frequently necessitate that individual desires will be frustrated for the sake of common satisfactions, as circumstances require. But the result is the most complete kind of satisfaction worthy of attainment by human beings. As Josiah Royce held, man is man by virtue of his mutually shared loyalties. Or, in Augustine's words, man is as he loves, with others, a common object.

The peculiar experiences which faith invests with highest value, then, are those which point beyond the affectivity of the individual centered self to the communion of centered selves in which he discovers himself and is enabled to develop both in his own centeredness and in his wider participation. As faith anticipates the future and assigns it a preeminent place in its scale of intrinsic values, the single most important contributor to the possibility of enhanced satisfaction, it begins also to conceive "future" as the future of the community of which each is a part. Every believer's future is inextricably bound to the future of a community because his worthwhile experiences are those which can occur only in the nurture of that community. Each has a value-laden future if and only if the community which sustains him persists as a community within which he will continue both to desire and to enjoy the satisfactions of those desires with others. The salvation of centered beings is into and of a community. In its most profound integration of a centered self's experiences by means of a scale of values, faith becomes a trusting in the promise of a significant future for and in the human community:

O blest communion, fellowship divine!
We feebly struggle, they in glory shine;
Yet . . . hearts are brave again, and arms are strong.
Alleluia! Alleluia!*

Hope of this sort is not merely an activity of worlded, centered beings focused only upon humanly contrived ideals. Faith hopes "in" a being believed to be the aim of all hope: a *guarantor* of a value-laden future, that is, of the persistence of all that contributes to maximum satisfactions of self-conscious beings. The very name God suggests how intimately bound in human consciousness are believing in God and hoping for the future: "I will be there." He who has created and is creating the possibility of the future himself will remain present to the human community as that community claims its future by achieving its possibilities in the present. When all beings have come to their appointed end, faith affirms, God himself will be in their midst, uniting them in ways which transcend all humanly envisioned worlds.

To gather these considerations into the form of a summary statement: Faith in God as the source of all being arises in and through man's attempts to achieve centeredness of being in a world whose constituents are primally understood as either threatening to or supportive of the coming-to-be of that centered self. It is one orientation, among many, toward man's situation. With all such orientations, it seeks to organize the totality of experience in such a way that centeredness is attained when desire is most fully satisfied. Faith's unique perspective on the human situation is that the possibility of centeredness is bestowed by a *transcendent guarantor* of man's life, "through all worlds." The future is the future for and of centered beings, whose worldedness enhances rather

* From the hymn "For All the Saints" by William W. How.

139

than limits the possibilities of centeredness. "God" is the name both of the source of that hope and the guarantor of the conditions under which the hope is to be realized.

The fundamental question about faith now becomes whether any good reasons can be cited, on independent grounds, for the assertions about reality which faith articulates from its profoundly hopeful state of mind. It is one thing to *yearn* for a significant future, to experience the *promise* of a significant future as a genuine possibility. Promise-makers abound in human life. But is there any reason to suppose that one could experience a promise-maker who is *sufficient* to ensure the yield of his promises? Can a case be made for supposing that man's most deep-seated wishes will indeed be fulfilled by a *transcendent* promise-maker, conceived after the fashion of an altogether benevolent human being?

Secular consciousness is more than willing to posit, even against all odds, that the human community itself will persist. Indeed, it seems at times that secular consciousness has never even considered the alternative possibility. And if the foregoing analysis of "thing-world" is sound, it is not absurd to suppose that all that transpires within the order of nature is precisely for the purpose of establishing the conditions for the persistence of the human community, not merely on this planet but throughout the universe. It should not now be as obvious as some would suppose that the world order is of everlasting duration and everlastingly oblivious to human life; the previous considerations should show that it is at least *as* intelligible to posit that nothing truly can be said to be at all in the finite order save as it impinges upon man, that throughout the whole of physical reality is manifest an evolutionary process which anticipates an everlasting community of conscious beings at its consummation. But it is not easy to believe that guaranteeing the evolutionary process, and in it man's most exalted expectations, is the power of a transcendent promise-maker and promise-keeper. How could one possibly infer, merely from the experience of a possibility, the existence of a *transcendent* bestower of that possibility? Merely by wishful thinking or longing? Or does faith itself yield some experiential basis for this further surmise? The following section seeks an answer to this question.

THE EXPERIENCE OF GOD IN FAITH

It must be noted at the outset that the experiential basis for faith cannot be regarded as providing proof for faith's claims. Faith cannot authenticate its affirmations about reality because it is not *primarily* a set of claims about reality at all; it is the expression of a hopeful and trusting human *response* to reality. Its mood of hopefulness is not achieved as a result of studied considerations; believers do not *conclude* that they ought to be hopeful from a dispassionate examination of evidence. Their hopefulness orients their experience wholly in advance of any serious attempt to determine whether or not hope is an appropriate attitude for man, given the nature of reality. Mere appeal to the experiential foundations for faith, then, will not settle the question of whether or not believers are deluded in their hoping, whether it is all made up in their imaginations that they live in a world about which human beings rightly can be hopeful. The fundamental reason why this is so is that the experiences from which faith arises do not include *immediate* experience of the reality named by the word God. The guarantor of the significant human future is not encountered directly, in the way that its mother's breast is encountered by a sucking infant. If there is actually a guarantor of man's future, as well as the possibility that there is, nothing in experience makes this obvious beyond all question; one can only *infer* such a reality on the basis of what human beings *do* experience. Close examination of the very meaning of "faith" should make plain the appropriateness of these comments. If human beings did experience God directly, and not merely intimations of a divine presence in finite reality, it would make no sense to speak of their existence as justified by faith; they would live by sight. In essence, faith is trusting in something for which there is *not* decisive evidence. Some have suggested even that faith calls for trusting in spite of the evidence. Experience of God is experiencing the possibility of a conscious, caring presence sufficiently endowed with resources to guarantee man's future. The possibility is suggested in and through the satisfactions of communal life, a sharing in an enhancing vision commanding mutual loyalty and obedience.

Though faith is not direct experience of God, however, it does include within its own inner dynamic a first set of rudimentary, vaguely articulated *inferences* from experience to a caring presence which transcends as well as evokes those experiences. Insofar as it is a hoping on the basis of perceptions intrinsically ambiguous in their representation of reality, perceptions which by no means make *plain* that hoping is in order, faith even in its most inchoate form involves some degree of hypothesizing on the basis of *possibilities* which appear to consciousness. Even in its least clarified expressions, faith is an attempt to conceptualize what that transcendent reality must be like for hoping to be fitting at all. In these senses, faith already is an attempt to achieve self-understanding. *Theology, as an understanding of faith, is only a further clarification of faith's own preliminary understanding of reality.*

The altogether crucial thesis which has been advanced through these pages is that the possibility of prayer rests upon the recovery of faith's own distinctive understanding of God, which all too frequently does *not* appear in traditional theological expositions of faith. What must appear to some as an unduly protracted examination of how faith

142

arises in self-conscious beings as one way of achieving orientation in the world, nevertheless was advanced as a theological inquiry into the fundamental dynamic of faith which *precedes* formulating a doctrine of God by means of another kind of theological reflection, that which often leads faith astray. The aim has been to theologize about the experience of faith which is *prior to* the kind of abstract theological thinking which has generated "orthodoxy," a tradition wrongly believed adequate to the faith it is supposed to represent. The question, frequently posed in these chapters, of how believers could subscribe to orthodox doctrines and continue to take prayer seriously now can be answered: Orthodox believers can pray because the faith by which they live is *not* in fact that with which orthodox doctrines have to do. Faith remains a primal world orientation which orthodoxy has yet to clarify.

Given the importance of the distinction, some further remarks are in order about the relationship between faith's own attempt to clarify its experience of God and theology's allegedly more precise interpretations of the prior and less clear understanding of faith itself. It seems evident that faith comes to expression partly through employing patterns of thinking which it does not fully understand but which it makes use of creatively, nevertheless. More specifically, faith portrays to itself the features of transcendent reality by means of a pattern of thinking whose fundamental presupposition is that there is something in common between the Transcendent and the beings of the world. Upon this supposition, faith speaks of God as the embodiment of the most supremely worthwhile experience and beings encountered in the world. The important point is that faith makes its supposition without consciously having before it any well-formed *doctrine* of thinking and knowing by which the supposition might be "justified." Faith *is* the supposing; it is *not* an enterprise primarily interested in providing either an account of or a justification for the supposing. Theology arises with the first interest in these latter sorts of questions.

If the account previously given of the origins of objectifying thinking is adequate, it ought to be possible to indicate now how theological thinking properly so-called emerges out of faith's prior and more basic way of thinking about reality. For it seems clear that theology objectifies the phenomenon of faith in ways analogous to metaphysical and scientific thinking's objectifying appearances which once impinged upon conscious beings in more primal ways. Interest in the doctrine by which faith thinks arises only when the thinking itself, for whatever reason, becomes questionable, when faith's primal relationship with its world breaks down. Then, "sound doctrine" also becomes an urgent concern, namely, an intellectual clarification of the beliefs faith implies, expressed in accordance with a rigorous methodology. Theologizing of these sorts indicates that faith has collided with alternative ways of experiencing the world and as a result is temporarily distracted from its own distinctive world orientation. (Whitehead once remarked that, wherever there is a creed, there is a heretic around the corner or in his grave.) To cope with this disruption in faith's orientation, theological thinking seeks, from a distance, to look *at* the phenomenon of faith, alongside those other ways of experiencing and interpreting reality different from that of the believing community. Though there is a natural proclivity toward theologizing in faith itself, the objectifying species of theological thinking arises primarily when faith momentarily is disoriented, weakened in its confidence about its own way of interpreting its world.

However objectifying it may become when at a distance from faith, theological reflection is one with that of faith at the level of common presupposition. Both seek to bring transcendent reality closer to consciousness by conceiving its features as akin to some of those in the

144

finite order, but in a perfectly embodied form. The adequacy of both is dependent upon the proper choice of the *kinds* of finite being with which God's own being is to be compared. Classical theology wrongly decided to be guided by human experience of a thing-world as the basis for its thinking about God and thereby came to portray the reality transcending the thing-world in thinglike terms. As has been argued previously, skill at interpreting experience according to categories definitive of a thing-world is not the kind of skill which faith needs for the sake of clarifying that ultimate reality to which it is a response. Objectifying thinking is a highly abstract pattern of conceptualizing about experiences which are far removed from those constituting conscious being's primary relationships with reality. In order genuinely to describe God as the transcendent guarantor of a significant human future, theological thinking must refer to the kinds of experiences which generate faith initially and seek to formulate its doctrine of God with those experiences alone in mind. The kind of experience which is of most fundamental importance for thinking about God is the experience of selves in community. It is only from these kinds of experiences that the question of God can be raised in a truly significant way: i.e., whether one can infer legitimately, from believing that one's future will be significant, a belief in a transcendent guarantor of the loving community which conditions any significant future for an individual. When the question of God is asked in this way, the *form* of the answer will rest upon certain discernments about the potentialities ingredient in interpersonal relationships, intersubjectivity. It is upon these sorts of discernments, and not those pertinent to the thing-world, that belief in God truly rests. (It is tempting to formulate this thesis by means of a widely employed concept in contemporary theology, "existential analogies." But, in the first place, it is not a species of analogical thinking which faith exhibits but rather one of *literal* thinking, what medieval theologians referred to as the way of *eminence*. Faith ascribes, literally and not analogically, characteristics of certain finite beings to God, insisting only that in God the highest conceivable finite characteristics are wholly and perfectly embodied. Secondly, even in the thinking of most for whom "existential analogies" are especially significant, human experience is wrongly conceived in highly individualized terms. For example, in Kierkegaard faith is one's own contemporaneity with Christ and in Bultmann it is an individual's response to a Word singularly addressed to him. Neither view is sufficiently clear about how communities, personal and otherwise, drastically condition the intrapsychic life of every individual, especially their highest moments of consciousness.)

Faith's primordial thinking about God is founded upon the discernment that every encounter with another self-conscious being is also an encounter with a dimension of value which transcends the one encountered. Faith is possible at all only for those who can see in every conscious relationship with another conscious being, and in every personal relationship with another personal being, intimations of significance vastly greater than that which the participants in such relationships bear. Those who discern the penumbral meanings coalescing around other selves have the capacity to become, or have already become, "believers." For God appears first and finally only in the company of some specific person or persons as that transcendent dimension of significance to whom every personal being points. God can encounter only those human beings who can envision, in and surrounding other human beings, a genuinely transcendent dimension of meaning greater than the totality of meaning presently apparent in and about the one(s) encountered.

For those with such "eyes to see," each relationship

does indeed suggest an infinitude of rich experiences yet to transpire, many of them beyond the capabilities of either to enjoy, but many also ready to be shared as each matures in personhood through encounters with still other selves. The spouse-to-be whom one greets at the altar or the infant first laid in his crib at his homecoming from the hospital discloses to all but the utterly insensitive a fullness of relationships to be enjoyed, but also presently beyond the capacity of each participant fully to appreciate.

Part of the transcendent significance of interpersonal relationships, then, derives merely from anticipating encounters yet to come. But the transcendent dimension also appears in the fullness of the present relationship, as each participant brings to it both his own being and a plenitude of being not strictly speaking his. As do spouses and infants, each person exhibits in his own being the impact and continuing presence of that wider community of selves to which both he and those encountering him belong. Each human being represents that body of countless and nameless individuals who, in contributing their own legacies to the human environing world, even now condition all that is authentically human in this and every subsequent age. In this sense, each human being bears enormous symbolic significance: He is an outward and visible sign of an invisible community's ongoing presence, whose influences continue to shape the possibilities for the present and the future. Every human being points beyond himself to unfathomable depths of relationships possible between human beings, an infinitude of mutually enhancing and satisfying experiences in community still to be delighted in.

But the richness of human relationships is, after all, beyond the capacity of any member of a community, and of the whole community itself, to experience. Those who are acutely sensitive to the inexhaustible possibilities of satisfying experiences in community also know of the ominous possibility of irrecoverable loss, the possibility that the infinitude of possible human experience may fail to be actualized because it encompasses a scope beyond finite capacities to assimilate. In the midst of precisely this kind of disturbing consideration, faith is the affirmation of an alternative possibility: that all that is beyond man's powers to experience is gathered and conserved in the experience of a transcendent Person for whom nothing can ever be lost. Faith's primal discernment of God, arising with the experience of transcendent dimensions of communal existence, is that "God" is the name of a being who embodies completely every personal quality, including especially the capacity to respond to and retain in his own conscious life the memory of every event, every experience, and every anticipation of both. In the midst of finite selves who experience themselves and others finitely, faith discerns the presence of One whose experience is of the whole of human reality, whose very nature is to assimilate its manifold impingements into his own consciousness in order to enrich his own life forever.

The experience of God is the experience of a personal being who is affected by and is responsive to the whole of the human self-world in ways not possible for any self within that world, whose capacities to be affected and to respond are by comparison infinitesimal. By their very nature, for finite conscious selves, excessive stimulation, by the impinging of too large a segment of an environment at once, paralyzes receptivity, with the result that consciousness becomes desensitized. By contrast, for God, nothing that anyone experiences fails either to have an effect or to be responded to. This is not to say that God's experiences are identical with what everyone experiences, or that anyone's experiences are genuine only as God, too, experiences them. Nor is it to suggest that the worthwhileness of human experience *is* its being experienced by God, as if man's future is merely as content in the divine consciousness. Every conscious being, both God and finite creatures, has *his* unique experiences which no one else can have in the same way. The worth of any such experience is a feature of that experience and not of someone else's having that experience. Neither God nor any other conscious being is enhanced by having experiences which, strictly speaking, are another's to have. It is no loss that God has his experiences and finite selves have theirs; the respective experiences *cannot* be identified if the selfhood of each is to be preserved. Faith in God's sufficiency is a trusting that nothing anyone ever experiences could fail to impinge upon the divine consciousness. What matters for faith is not that God have as his own the experiences of others but that God's own being can be *affected* by them, that each creature can make a genuine impact upon *his* creator.

The point under consideration is that faith becomes a possibility first in the experience of self-conscious beings in interpersonal situations. In these situations, faith discerns transcendent dimensions which include the possibility of a transcendent Person in whose consciousness all that finite beings are unable to experience is cherished forever. The understanding of God as that transcendent Person is to be developed always and only by means of images drawn from the person-world rather than from the thing-world of cause and effect. To speak of God as stilling storms in response to prayer is to mire faith in imagery which defies serious attention. It does not serve the cause of faith to speak of God's worldly activities as a direct impingement upon the natural order in this sense. What can be said of the divine impingement, instead, is that "it" is like that of a person, always upon the interpersonal existence of conscious selves. God is not a causal agent; he is a personal presence. His "effects" are not in a thing-world, unexpected alterations in the uniform sequences of events in that thing-world ("signs and wonders"). Instead he is to be experienced as a caring embrace, of and in a person-world, which persists in and through every vicissitude of life. God does not still storms; he quiets man's unholy terror of them. God is that One who never fails to be affirmative of every striving of human beings toward full personhood; in his solicitude, he affects the created order primarily by energizing resources within human beings which were not perceived to be available. It is in this light that the understanding of intercessory prayer previously elaborated has developed. One who makes requests before the "throne of grace" receives sufficient power himself to be the agent of God's response to the one prayed for. Once impotent to meet the other's need, he is now himself the presence of God to the other.

Properly to think about God, then, is to conceive God's relationship to the world to be like the impingement of one person upon another, not like the impingement of one thing upon another thing. It is like the nurture of a parent, and perhaps even of a friend, rather than like the collision of one billiard ball with another. To think about God as the "source of all there is" is to think of the *provider of the environing world within which human beings become persons in mutual relationship.* Faith's primordial understanding of God is in relation not to a thing-world but to the self-conscious beings whose source he is. He is addressed, boldly, as "Father" because he is the ground and the end of personal self-consciousness, the *supremely* personal being. Infinitely personal, he nonetheless is *a* person. The limitlessness of his personhood consists only in the degree of his power to be affected by the totality of human possibilities and experiences, a power infinitely greater than that of any finite sentient being, who cannot assimilate even his own possibilities, much less *all* possibilities. However tempting it may seem, presumably in the interest of accentuating the divine holiness, to conceive of God's personhood in utterly transcendent

150

terms, as if human language about persons applies *merely* symbolically, to do so is to define faith's discernments away rather than to interpret them insightfully. However "heavenly" God's fatherhood may be in comparison with that of even the most successful of earth's fathers, it is still *fatherly;* all that is *conceivably* good (viz., relevant to satisfying experiences) about human fathers defines precisely the content of man's idea of God. Only to such a personal being could faith sensibly address heartfelt prayers. And it is to just such a being that one *does* address any prayer that could matter to him.

To this point, then, the specter of cosmological naïveté should have been laid to rest with the insistence that *cosmic* facts are irrelevant to the question of the reality of God; faith claims only to experience a source of *personal* existence. Likewise, by likening God's relationship to the world to that of a *personal presence* rather than to that of a *causal agent,* the difficulties of believing in interventionism, previously defined, seem also to have been sufficiently minimized. But the anthropomorphism which permeates the proffered interpretation of God requires a defense which, strictly speaking, has yet to be given. For there is still a considerable difference between believing that the human community might have a significant future and believing that there is a personal guarantor of that future who is able to ensure it. While by definition faith does not conclude the latter from the former on the basis of carefully considering evidence, it does suppose that it has indeed rightly discerned what in fact is the case. For those who see the matter otherwise, it ought to be possible for faith to defend the adequacy of its powers of discernment by citing at least *some* reasons which could be given for this affirmation, on grounds independent of the experience of faith itself. It cannot be of service to the secular believer to portray the life of faith as analogous to the leap into a volcano which Empedocles allegedly made to end dramatically his philosophical career. To this final task, the chapter, and this study, now turn.

ON THE REASONABLENESS
OF FAITH IN GOD

There are two kinds of reasons which support believing in God as the personal ground and end of man's future. Neither presupposes the peculiar experiences which faith claims to have of God, the veridicality of which is the very point at issue. One is psychosocial in character; its premises derive from an examination of the inner dynamic of human personality and the ways in which society conditions its development. The other is ontological, based upon an understanding of a feature of being-as-such, of anything that is. Each now must be discussed in turn.

The psychosocial reasons for believing in God derive from the mounting evidence that personal self-consciousness is actualized only in encounters with other persons. Upon the basis of this kind of evidence, it is plausible to infer the presence of a transcendent Person as a way of accounting for the emergence of persons in a world which otherwise would contain only subpersonal beings. Many would now agree that what alone occasions genuinely personal growth is the impingement of other conscious beings who also are maturing as persons. Unless one can explain the phenomenon of personhood in terms merely of stimulus-response, analogous to cause-effect interactions in a world of things, whenever there is one person, there must be also the effective presence of at least two others. To become a person, each conscious individual requires significant and caring responses to his being by someone other than himself. That other person, however, cannot be capable of the requisite caring unless he in turn has been cared for by still another, and so on. All of which should suggest that personal self-consciousness cannot be accounted for by reference merely to antecedent circumstances; though the chain of personal encounters projected backward through time points to the subpersonal, the basic components of personal existence cannot have evolved *merely* from the subpersonal. For the personal to emerge from the subpersonal, what is required is the impingement of a person already transcending the subpersonal world. For faith, that transcendent Person is what is meant by "God," the eminent person to whom all beings point and whose own higher order of being the subpersonal cannot ever by itself come to emulate.

To be sure, personal self-consciousness is also dependent upon the coalescing of certain purely physical conditions which themselves are explicable wholly by reference to antecedent circumstances: for example, the formation of an atmosphere with the requisite proportion of oxygen to nitrogen and carbon dioxide. However, from such conditions alone, only *living* beings could be said to evolve, some of which in addition possess *consciousness*. The laws in accordance with which physical phenomena evolve into living organisms and into conscious living beings do not account in addition for the emergence of that altogether different kind of embodied reality which is *personal* being. They do not explain the emergence of *personal* centers of consciousness in mere conscious beings, many of whom are clearly incapable of the kind of caring which constitutes decidedly personal existence.

From the standpoint of evolutionary theory, even though several of its supporting conditions can be shown to have considerable survival value, the development of personal self-consciousness from those supporting conditions seems by contrast utterly maladaptive. To elaborate, personal self-consciousness cannot develop at all unless there is already present in an organism the capacity to differentiate individual members of its species; a being incapable of discriminating within its species cannot de-

153

velop personal relationships with others of its own kind. More primitive sentient beings appear to distinguish, at best, only their own species from other species; while they apparently are able to recognize that another is of their own kind, they cannot discern anything important about that other by which to differentiate it from others like it. During the course of organic evolution, cognitive power appears to develop in some species to far more complex levels; individuals of those species come to distinguish and remember other individuals *within* their own species. It is this higher power of discrimination which is indispensable for the emergence of *self*-consciousness. Self-consciousness requires the capacity to recognize another as a conscious center, over against which and alongside of which one comes to understand *himself,* a phenomenon present to himself in his consciousness of others like himself. But the further refinement of self-conscious beings into *persons* cannot be accounted for by these same antecedent conditions. However exalted the love relationship has been in Western culture, from an evolutionary standpoint it is disfunctional and hence ought not to survive. Positing conscious care for another individual's welfare as the highest expression of conscious existence, the norm for all relationships among conscious beings, negates evolutionary principles determinative for a billion years (give or take 500 million). So to care requires unlearning (if that is possible) patterns of behavior (arising out of what for some is an "aggressive instinct") whose primary purpose is to create significant *distance* between individuals, ensuring that members of a species, including the human, shall be equitably distributed across the given environment for maximum survival potential. The important exceptions to this pattern of behavior, in members of herds, do not constitute significant data against the thesis being argued for, since herds preclude both individuality and caring personal relationships almost universally. In the light of such ages-old mechanisms, how is it possible both to interpret the rise of and to posit a significant future for personal self-consciousness except by appeal to an impingement upon the evolutionary process of a personal self-consciousness sovereign over the evolutionary dynamic in that process?

It cannot be denied that this kind of reasoning by itself is incomplete. That personal self-conciousness appears maladaptive could indicate merely that it is one among many mutations which will assume no significance whatever in the evolutionary process as a whole. The psychosocial evidence establishes, if anything at all, only the existence of some personal being other than man who is conscious of, responsive to, and capable of influencing the course of physical evolution. It does not show also that that personal being is capable of experiencing, sustaining, and responding to the *entirety* of human hopes and longings. A being like any of the Olympian pantheon, for instance, is all that would be required fully to account for personal self-consciousness. In this sense, the psychosocial "argument" shares the same deficiency characterizing all empirical arguments for God; it does not establish the existence of a being with *all* of the features exhibited by the Christian idea of God. The haunting doubt remains that a God unable to respond to all experience may not be sufficient to guarantee the human future. To rephrase an ancient doctrine: That which God cannot experience, he cannot save. Finally, the reasoning is based upon at least two assumptions which are by no means self-evident: (1) that there is something qualitatively distinct about conscious personal beings from all that is either nonconscious or conscious but impersonal (i.e., an autistic child) and (2) that one cannot account for the appearance of a human environing world composed of conscious beings except

155

by reference to the impingement of a being of the same order.

Before dismissing the psychosocial considerations altogether, however, it is important to take into account another and supplementary kind of reasoning which is ontological in form. The relevant argument from ontology begins with the observation, previously elaborated, that there is in the human community a degree of potential experience which no individual in the community is capable of having, and which the whole community itself cannot enjoy, given that its members are finite individually and that their totality is a finite totality. No individual can experience actually all that he is aware of as possible, nor can any community do so. Along with this consideration, a certain ontological hypothesis also is relevant: that *the very meaning of the term possibility requires the notion of actualization under some conditions at some time.* If this hypothesis is sound, and there are many responsible thinkers who believe that it is, then whatever one would mean by "this or that possibility," he must intend to refer to, and be able to conceive of, some actualizable state of affairs. More precisely, to speak intelligibly of possibility x or possibility y, one must be able to state the *conditions under which x or y could be actualized*, if not in the present at least at some future time. Negatively put, the hypothesis is that it is self-contradictory to speak of an x as possible if by definition that x could never be actualized under any condition at any time. Thus, the strange expression "round square" expresses an *impossible* state of affairs.

The argument on the basis of the foregoing premises now can be advanced. Human beings interpret their experience as including the genuine possibility of an inexhaustively rich conscious personal experience in unending relationship with other selves. If the idea of such a possibility is a coherent idea, as it appears to be on the surface, the ontological hypothesis dictates that there must be some conscious being who is the subject of such experience, who is genuinely affected by every relationship which transpires in a personal world; *only* such a being could constitute the condition for the possibility to be actualized. Faith names that being "God." Upon this reasoning, belief in God is one way of expressing the conditions under which the human environing world could be experienced and responded to in its totality.

There is much about this line of argument, too, which is fraught with difficulty. For instance, and especially, every occurrence of evil in the world seems to count extraordinarily heavily against believing in God so conceived. How could a God whose sensitive caring constitutes his very essence, and whose sufficiency is faith's essential affirmation, be affected by the enormity of human frustration and not enter into the very situations which occasion the frustrations for the sake of altering them directly? Can belief in the incarnation overcome this difficulty? A further difficulty has to do with the intelligibility of believing that man's highest conceived values cannot fail to be actualized, when with every passing moment the number of values not actualized increases demonstrably. It cannot be a "comfortable doctrine" that God *alone* experiences all that human beings fail to experience, for then it would follow that the only sort of being important for man is for *God* to experience him. Clearly, this is not the kind of significant future which faith envisions. Finally, one can doubt the adequacy of the interpretation of human existence which posits an infinite richness to potential experiences, even if one cannot doubt the soundness of the ontological principle itself. Many conscious beings, who otherwise might be deemed "persons," do not appear to encounter others as laden with infinite import. The persistent tendency of human beings to depersonalize others starkly implies that the personal environing world might be quite different from what it has been alleged to be during the course of this exposition. (Although, it must be noted, the argument previously elaborated requires only the existence of *one* person as its basis, not the existence of a human community within which personhood is universally acknowledged.)

However, while these premises, which constitute the precise burden which must be sustained in order to make a *case* for believing in God, may not be indubitably certain, they do seem plausible. By appealing to them, one can legitimately speak not only of valid arguments for faith's God but of sound arguments as well, in that conclusions can be drawn, with formal correctness, on the basis of beliefs for which there is at least *some* evidence. And whatever difficulties may attend this entire line of reasoning, it does reduce considerably the force of the opposition to anthropomorphic thinking in faith. Traditionally, as has been elaborated previously, that argument is that an anthropomorphically conceived God is no more than an ideal state of *human* existence wrongly believed to be embodied in a transcendent being. But according to the foregoing analysis, the perfect state conceivable by men is *never* achievable by human beings, because the human community can entertain ideal possibilities that it itself can never actualize. No conception of human achievement permits supposing that at some future time anyone in the human community, or even the whole community itself, could experience all of the mutually enhancing relationships conceivable by human beings. Thus, it would appear altogether appropriate for man to posit a transcendent Person responsive to the whole of the person-world. There is no religious consolation in an ideal conception of human life which includes within it the understanding that nothing in all creation is capable of actualizing the ideal of an infinitude of mutually enhancing relationships. Alternatively, faith boldly affirms that man's profoundest hopes are fulfilled in the life of a *transcendent* being. Faith knows that there is no consummation of those hopes *except* by such. Rather than a naïve and crude product of wish fulfillment, anthropomorphic thinking reflects the most deep-going articulation of the most mature understanding of human possibilities and their grounding in the order of being generally. That faith and prayer require anthropomorphic language is to the credit of faith and to the embarrassment of neither.

With this defense of the final conviction upon which prayer depends, this present study justifiably comes to a close. The aim of these chapters has been to reopen the possibility of prayer for those whose faith seemed questionable in the light of a secular orientation toward life, whose own validity many believers rightly are unwilling to deny. If the argument has succeeded, then searching, secular-minded men and women should be able to incorporate with utmost seriousness a secular world view into the inner dynamic of an unashamedly faith-filled response to that same reality which calls both secularity and faith to be. One result should be that they will find it possible again to pray, if not without ceasing, then certainly earnestly and with a vigor from which genuine works of love and service can proceed, to the glory of God the Father in worlds without end.

ABOUT THE AUTHOR

Leroy T. Howe, a native of Coral Gables, Florida is an ordained minister of the United Methodist Church. He is associate dean and associate professor of philosophical theology at Perkins School of Theology of Southern Methodist University, Dallas, Texas.

Dr. Howe has been a Rockefeller Brothers Theological Fellow and a Woodrow Wilson Fellow and holds degrees from the University of Miami (A.B., M.A.), Yale Divinity School (B.D.) and Yale University (M.A., Ph.D.). Dr. and Mrs. Howe are the parents of two daughters, Jennifer and Allison, and live in Richardson, Texas.